Holy Ground

Holy Ground

A Gathering of Voices on
Caring for Creation

Edited by Lyndsay Moseley
and the staff of Sierra Club Books

Foreword by Carl Pope

SIERRA CLUB BOOKS
San Francisco

The Sierra Club, founded in 1892 by author and conservationist John Muir, is the oldest, largest, and most influential grassroots environmental organization in the United States. With more than a million members and supporters—and some sixty chapters across the country—we are working hard to protect our local communities, ensure an enduring legacy for America's wild places, and find smart energy solutions to stop global warming. To learn how you can participate in the Sierra Club's programs to explore, enjoy, and protect the planet, please address inquiries to Sierra Club, 85 Second Street, San Francisco, California 94105, or visit our website at www.sierraclub.org.

The Sierra Club's book publishing division, Sierra Club Books, has been a leading publisher of titles on the natural world and environmental issues for nearly half a century. We offer books to the general public as a nonprofit educational service in the hope that they may enlarge the public's under-standing of the Sierra Club's concerns and priorities. The point of view expressed in each book, however, does not necessarily represent that of the Sierra Club. For more information on Sierra Club Books and a complete list of our titles and authors, please visit www.sierraclub.org/books.

Published by Sierra Club Books
85 Second Street, San Francisco, CA 94105

Sierra Club Books are published in association with Counterpoint (www.counterpointpress.com).

SIERRA CLUB, SIERRA CLUB BOOKS, and the Sierra Club design logos are registered trademarks of the Sierra Club.

Project editor for Sierra Club Books: Diana Landau
Book and jacket design: Linda Herman, Glyph Publishing Arts

Library of Congress Cataloging-in-Publication Data

Holy ground: a gathering of voices on caring for creation / edited by Lyndsay Moseley and the staff of Sierra Club Books; foreword by Carl Pope.
    p. cm.
  ISBN 978-1-57805-160-1 (cloth : alk. paper)
  I. Nature--Religious aspects. 2. Ecotheology. 3. Human ecology—Religious aspects.
I. Moseley, Lyndsay
  BL65.N35H65 2008
  261.8'8--dc22   2008034039

Printed in the United States of America on Cascades Enviro 100 acid-free paper, which contains 100 percent post-consumer waste, processed chlorine free

Distributed by Publishers Group West
12 11 10 09 08
10 9 8 7 6 5 4 3 2 1

Contents

Editors' Preface

Nearly two decades ago, a group of renowned scientists, including Dr. Carl Sagan and thirty-two other Nobel laureates, wrote an open letter to religious leaders. In it they acknowledged the limits of science and technology in changing attitudes and behaviors that were contributing to massive environmental degradation. The scientists called the environmental crisis "intrinsically religious" and sought "joint cause and action" with the world's religious leaders.

They were breaking ground, and so were the theologians and religious leaders who began in the 1950s and '60s to explore the connections between theology and ecology. While those connections can be traced back thousands of years—to the foundational texts of nearly every major world religion—not until fairly recently did many people begin to consider issues such as pollution, endangered species, and global warming from a faith perspective.

But even amid these explorations in the last century, the environment came to be seen as a divisive political cause championed by liberals, while religious voices in the public square became increasingly allied with conservative politics.

Growing up in a deeply religious and politically conservative family in eastern Tennessee, I felt this tension directly. Our home was situated along the Fort Loudon Reservoir of the Tennessee River, in the foothills of the Great Smoky Mountains. We had a small garden of tomatoes and cucumbers, neighboring woods and cow fields to play in, and a shallow inlet on the reservoir that turned to mudflats when the water level was lowered for winter. I often wandered down to a small dock, where I found a strong sense of myself and of God's presence while watching fish jump and spiders dart about on the water's surface. But I would never have labeled myself an environmentalist.

In high school, while attending the Youth Theology Institute at Emory University's Candler School of Theology, I first realized the power of faith to shape public life and policy. Faith as a mode and motivator of public engagement intrigued me, and in graduate school I found my way into a job doing research on faith-based environmental activism in southern Appalachia. I began to read about the bonds between ecology and theology on an abstract level, but as I began to feel this connection personally and spiritually, I was inspired to get back out into nature. Each step in my journey felt providential, carrying me forward with an unfolding sense of calling.

In a class on community organizing, I encountered an especially heartbreaking case of pollution in a low-income community outside Knoxville. Drinking water had been contaminated by the illegal dumping of toxics, including lead, arsenic, diesel fuel, and PCBs. This seemed such a clear example of "creation groaning," as in the verse from Romans (8:22) that says, "For we know that the whole creation groans and travails in pain together." It brought home to me once and for all the idea that environmental quality and the quality of human life are inextricable. Taking part in a coalition of residents, union leaders, environmentalists, and church folks to demand clean water for the neighborhood, I discovered how citizen action can bring victory against tremendous odds. And as I saw how the fate of that Knoxville community was joined to the fate of the Earth, I began to understand that God's call to care for creation is the same as God's call to love our neighbors. Closing the circle, I volunteered at my church to help raise awareness of biblical teachings on stewardship; leading others to this awakening was another kind of victory.

The recognition of shared values has great power to shape society. Thanks to the vision and leadership of many of this book's contributors—and countless others—more and more people of faith are connecting deeply held religious values of stewardship, justice, mindfulness of future generations, and various forms of the call to "love your neighbor" directly to environmental concerns. And religious engagement in environmental conversations provides much-needed opportunities to recalibrate expectations, lay down preconceived notions, and redefine our views on stewardship.

The Sierra Club seeks to be a "big tent," bringing people from diverse backgrounds together to seek solutions. Given this, and given that nearly half of the organization's members attend worship services regularly, it was a natural step for the Sierra Club to seek partnerships with people who espouse faith-based, moral, or spiritual reasons for protecting the Earth. This has been the focus of my work since 2005. Partnership does not imply a wholesale endorsement of any particular leader, tradition, or set of teachings, but rather a search for intersecting values. We aim to build strong relationships based on trust, enhanced understanding, and a willingness to work together. In the process, we often find things we must agree to disagree on, but we are learning to see the world and each other more completely and more compassionately.

The long-held idea that God created the Earth to be exploited for human advancement is no longer accepted without qualification. People of faith are coming to the table as strong allies in working to protect the planet; barriers and stereotypes are being replaced by respect and collaboration. We hope for and envision a world in which we can transcend our differences for the greater good. This book is no small expression of that hope.

Organizations like the National Religious Partnership for the Environment, along with a whole cadre of theologians and religious leaders, have given much attention to shaping religious engagement around key theological principles and moral and spiritual values. Less attention has been paid to how these values and principles become part of the core convictions of local leaders and congregants. So one of our chief aims in requesting pieces for this book was to encourage leaders from many faith traditions to share personal stories of how they experience creation, how they came to understand humankind's unique power and responsibility for its care, and how they pass that understanding on to those they lead.

My colleagues and I were pleased when Sierra Club Books supported the idea of a book that would speak not just to the religious groups we partner with but also to a broad general audience. In assembling this collection, I was fortunate to work closely with Sierra Club Books' acting editorial director, Diana Landau, who previews some of the contents below.

As Sierra Club founder John Muir said long ago, "Everyone needs beauty as well as bread, places to play in and pray in where nature may heal body and soul alike." Whether you read this collection on your own or with friends, we hope you are nourished and challenged by these stories, and moved to see the power of bringing together caring people of all faiths and all beliefs to protect our common holy ground.

—*Lyndsay Moseley*

This collection arose from the remarkable work of the Sierra Club's faith partnerships initiative. Lyndsay Moseley and her colleagues wished for a volume of readings that could reflect the ferment of thinking and activity on the part of faith groups coming to grips with the spiritual imperative of Earth stewardship—a book they could use in their outreach to such groups, and that religious groups themselves could use for classes and discussions.

The project captured my intense interest, as an editor with a bent for writing that explores the spiritual dimensions of the created world and as a recently reengaged Episcopalian. Long dismayed by the divide between so-called conservatives and progressives that seemed to trap the public voice of religion on one side, I had been opened to a more spacious understanding of Jesus's teachings by my own church and encouraged by signs that the moral urgency of stewardship was becoming a topic of religious discourse.

So we set to work, aiming, as Lyndsay notes, for a collection of writings in which faith leaders from many traditions could speak directly and personally to their followers and to all readers. Not every candidate we approached was at liberty to contribute, but to our delight, we received engaging writings from the Ecumenical Patriarch Bartholomew and Pope Benedict XVI, leaders respectively of the eastern and western branches of

Christianity, and from the leader of one evangelical "megachurch," Joel C. Hunter—among other important contributors.

Most of the voices in this collection are from Judeo-Christian backgrounds, but we also sought to represent Muslim, Hindu, Buddhist, and Native American perspectives. In addition, we wished to tap the deep strain of nature writing that finds the divine manifested in the physical world. Sierra Club Books is a leading publisher in this tradition, and we are pleased that the collection includes some of its contemporary masters, Gary Snyder, Wendell Berry, and Terry Tempest Williams among them.

Talking with contributors, we suggested themes that might emerge: the biblical call to stewardship, the concept of creation "groaning" under its burden of abuse, our human relationship with animals, and the growing movement for environmental justice as an expression of the commandment to love others as oneself. The voices gathered here speak about all of these and much more. In many of the writings, we encounter a fundamental and profound recognition that creation is supremely good, that we humans were endowed with paradise, that morality is built into creation. This seems to be an insight often sparked in childhood—Phyllis Tickle, Ingrid Mattson, and Joel Hunter all note it—and that grows in power with maturity and study. Similarly, other writers discern an intrinsic harmony in the natural world, a thread that runs through many traditions, from Navajo spirituality to Zen; Linda Hogan and Bishop Mark MacDonald illuminate such indigenous perspectives.

Some contributors, including Cal DeWitt, Benedict, and Zoë Klein, interpret the messages about stewardship contained in scripture and sacred story—starting with the Genesis charge to humankind. Others explore the imagery and meaning of water (Larry Rasmussen on baptism); of trees as rooted angels or messengers, living things that reach to heaven (Rabbi Waskow and Imam Shakir); or of animals as our companions on Earth or exemplars of sacrifice (Janisse Ray and David James Duncan). Gary Snyder reminds us of the universal obligation to give thanks for our sustenance, the grace by which we live.

Many of the writers here point to the life and teachings of Jesus: his baptism, his testing in the wilderness, his garden parables, and especially his exalting of the poor and marginalized. Contemplating his message in an age of climate change can bring new insight both to environmentalists and to those who perceive "the environment" chiefly as a political movement. It helps us all understand that the great commandment to care for our neighbor is now a global imperative—and one that cannot be fulfilled in the absence of caring for creation. Wendell Berry's readings of the Samaritan story and of Jesus's promise of "abundant life" enlarge our perception of the Gospel, while Kristin Shrader-Frechette's memoir of her family and career shatters the boundaries around whom and what we should care for.

People affiliated with religious institutions are people sworn and schooled to put their beliefs into practice. Idaho pastor Tri Robinson recounts his childhood experience of wilderness camping and his adult recognition of paradise lost; going off to meditate in his personal wilderness, he emerged with a vigorous new environmental mission for his Vineyard Church congregation. Several other contributors also share their "on the ground" experiences of working for change: Sally Bingham writes about bringing green energy to American churches, David Radcliff about introducing young people to endangered cultures and creatures worldwide, and Peter Sawtell about building hopeful activism in congregations.

We hope this small book will open many more doors to insight, conversation, and action. In a world too often polarized by beliefs and causes, the pilgrimage of environmentalists and people of faith toward common ground is a stirring sign of hope. There may yet be misunderstandings and tensions, but surely the presence within these covers of so many writers of such diverse beliefs is good news. Without a deeply felt spiritual basis for the sacrifices involved in becoming a planetary community—another way of saying we are all children of God—we cannot care for creation. And without creation, our human souls are homeless.

—*Diana Landau*

Foreword

A True Vocation

Carl Pope

This book is intended to inspire, to comfort, to connect. For these are the works of faith, and we offer here faith made tangible in words, expressed in the understandings of the great traditions, seeking nurturance from the Earth.

My first encounter with the intersection of faith and the environment came ten years ago in Santa Barbara. At a symposium hosted by the Ecumenical Patriarch Bartholomew—leader of the Orthodox Church and the first voice in this volume— I confessed that my generation of environmentalists had sinned. In the heady aftermath of the first Earth Day, we had walked away from the churches, the synagogues, the mosques, and the temples—from the very institutions to which millions of people turn when seeking to live out their deepest values—and we thereby risked turning the environmental ethic into an environmental subculture.

The decade since then has been a fearful time for faith and for the Earth. The Sierra Club has been accused, perhaps justly, of dwelling too darkly on the challenges and threats that modern society's exercise of power without wisdom has unleashed.

But we are not alone in our anxiety. Last September I stood on the deck of the ship *Fram*, in Erik's Fjord, south Greenland, among what was perhaps the most diverse group ever gathered on that coast, for a weeklong scientific and religious symposium on global warming. I listened as Patriarch Bartholomew warned us that climate change is our time's *kairos*, a Greek term for a moment of eternal consequence. A *kairos*, Bartholomew said, makes its own demands—demands we are not free to ignore. We do not have time, he warned, to balance the need for action against its possible risks. "The sea is warming, the ice is melting, and the catastrophe already visiting the Arctic will not stop here."

He closed with: "God grant us the wisdom to act in time."

A year earlier, at the Festival of Hearts in San Francisco, I was privileged to share the first deep encounter between the leaders of Islam and the Dalai Lama—the world's most rigorously monotheistic faith in dialogue with religion's least theistic leader. I expected, and heard, urgent appeals concerning the need for peace and reconciliation. I did not expect the frank assessment offered by one of the Muslim leaders, and agreed to by all, that "all of the world's faiths need each other, for time is not on their side. The modern's world's new god is commercialism, and the shopping mall is its altar."

Listening, I wondered: is it possible that, in the end, the great choice lies between the conjoined traditions of faith and reverence for the Earth, opposed to the forces of commercialism and acquisition? The idea intrigued and reassured me.

But there is a danger in this seeming unison of voices. We may take from it merely reassurance that our concerns are validated because they are shared by others—that we have new "allies," and that our values, even if making scant headway against the acquisitive tides of modern life, are nonetheless true and right.

That is sentimentality, not faith. Faith is demanding. It summons us to act. It demands that belief be tested by practice, hope tempered by struggle, dreams painfully worked into reality. It may demand that we acknowledge when we've strayed.

After I had made my confession at the Santa Barbara meeting all those years ago, a Greek Orthodox bishop, his black robes set off with silver crosses, approached me. In a deep voice he said heavily, "You know what comes after confession. Penance." He said it as a statement.

"I'll be glad to climb Mount Athos, even on my knees," I smiled in return.

Doing penance for Earth can and should be a joy. Perhaps not always the kind of "no pain, no gain," endorphin-producing joy of a steep climb; nonetheless, our best values and our souls' well-being may require a brisk workout to challenge our complacency. We hope this volume will help sustain you on that journey. As the Presbyterian minister and writer Frederick Buechner said, true vocation is where "your deep gladness and the world's deep hunger meet." We all need such a vocation.

Journey well.

Carl Pope is executive director of the Sierra Club and has served the organization for some thirty years. A veteran leader in the environmental movement, he has helped to build bridges to faith communities and other groups whose values are shared by environmentalists, and he is active on many boards. He is coauthor, with Paul Rauber, of Strategic Ignorance: Why the Bush Administration Is Recklessly Destroying a Century of Environmental Progress *(2004); his other books include* Sahib, an American Misadventure in India *(1971) and* Hazardous Waste in America *(1981).*

Introduction

Daring to Dream

Religion and the Future of the Earth

Mary Evelyn Tucker

There is a dawning realization from many quarters that the changes humans are making on the planet are comparable to the changes of a major geological era. The scientific evidence says that we are damaging life systems on Earth and causing species extinction (twenty thousand species lost annually) at such a rate as to bring about the end of our current period, the Cenozoic era. No such mass extinction has occurred since the dinosaurs were eliminated by an asteroid 65 million years ago.

Our period is considered to be the sixth major extinction in Earth's 4.7-billion-year history, and in this case humans are the primary cause. Having grown from 2 billion to 6 billion people in the twentieth century, we are now a planetary presence devouring resources and destroying ecosystems and biodiversity at an unsustainable rate. The data keeps pouring in that we are toxifying the air, water, and soil to such an extent that the health of all species is at risk. Global warming is already evident in melting glaciers, thawing tundra, and flooding coastal regions.

This increasing damage to ecosystems reveals that we are making macrophase changes to the planet with microphase wisdom. We are not fully aware of the scale of the damage we are doing, and we are not yet capable of stemming the tide of destruction.

For decades, environmental issues were considered the concern only of scientists, lawyers, and policy makers. Now the ethical dimensions of the environmental crisis are becoming more obvious. What is our moral responsibility toward future generations? How can we ensure equitable development that does not destroy the environment? Can religious and cultural perspectives help solve environmental challenges?

Among environmentalists, a conviction deepens: though science and policy approaches are clearly necessary, they are not sufficient to do the job of transforming human consciousness and behavior for a sustainable future. Values and ethics, religion and spirituality, are important factors in this transformation.

In 1947, historian Arnold Toynbee declared, "The twentieth century will be chiefly remembered by future generations not as an era of political conflicts or technical innovations but as an age in which human society dared to think of the welfare of the whole human race as a practical objective."

We might expand Toynbee's powerful statement to declare that the twenty-first century will be remembered by the extension of our moral concerns not only to humans but to other species and ecosystems as well—the Earth community as a whole. From social justice to eco-justice, the movement of human care pushes out in ever-widening concentric circles. The future of our withering planet, a commitment to its protection and restoration, may depend on the largeness of our embrace.

Our challenge now is to identify the vision and values that will spark a movement toward creating such a planetary civilization. A sustainable future requires not just managerial or legislative approaches—the saving of forests or fisheries—but a vision of that future, evoking depths of empathy, compassion, and sacrifice for the welfare of future generations. We are called to a new intergenerational consciousness and conscience.

Currently we in the developed world are easily distracted from these tasks by mass consumerism, media entertainment, and political manipulation. Our plundering power is almost invisible to the majority of people in the world, who are intent simply on feeding their families or, in affluent regions, on acquiring more goods. We need a serious wake-up call from our slumbers.

But solutions must inspire participation and action rather than frighten or disempower people. The next generation is searching for ways to contribute to a positive future. Life in all its variety and beauty calls to us for a response—a new integrated understanding of who we are as humans. This is not only about stewardship of the Earth but also about embracing our embeddedness in nature in radical, fresh, and enlivening ways. Humans, Earth, and the rest of life are bound in a single story and destiny. It is no longer a question of "saving the environment" as if it were something out there apart from us. We humans *are* the environment, and it is us—shaping our minds, nourishing our bodies, refreshing our spirit.

The task of articulating an integrated vision and identifying effective values requires new language, broader framing, inspiring images, captivating metaphors, and, most of all, new stories and dreams. As cultural historian Thomas Berry says, "If a society's cultural world—the dreams that have guided it to a certain point—become dysfunctional, the society must go back and dream again."

Currently the dreaming meets an impasse. There's a puzzling disconnection between our growing awareness of environmental problems and our ability to change our present direction. We have failed to translate facts about the environmental crisis into effective action in the United States. We are discovering that the human heart is not changed by facts alone but by engaging visions and empowering values. Humans need to see the large picture and feel they can act to make a difference.

We could name many complex factors that have contributed to this impasse, the failure of dreams. But despite frustrating trends, hopeful dreams are stirring, especially within religious communities.

Until recently, religious communities have been so absorbed in internal sectarian affairs that they have been unaware of the magnitude of the environmental crisis at hand. To be sure, the natural world figures prominently in the major religions: God's creation of material reality in Judaism, Christianity, and Islam; the manifestation of the divine in the karmic processes underlying the recycling of matter in Hinduism and Jainism; the interdependence of life in Buddhism; and the Tao (the Way) that courses through nature in Confucianism and Taoism. Despite those rich themes regarding nature, many religions turned from the turbulent world in a redemptive flight to a serene, transcendent afterlife.

Wanted: A New Ontology

But some within religious traditions, such as Thomas Berry, do acknowledge the urgency of our present moment. His concern, which is arising in religious and environmental circles alike, is whether humans are indeed a viable species—whether our presence on the planet is sustainable. As Metropolitan John of Pergamon, the Greek Orthodox theologian, has written, the problem is not simply about creating a stewardship ethic in which humans "manage" the Earth. Rather, he suggests, the current crisis challenges us to reformulate our ontology, our very nature as humans. How do we belong to this vast unfolding universe?

We need not deny the limits or the intolerant dimensions of religions that erupt in sectarianism and violence. However, religions have notably contributed to liberating movements for social justice and human rights. Religions demonstrate that they can change over time, transforming themselves and their dogma in response to new ideas and circumstances. Christian churches in Britain and the United States came to embrace the abolitionist movement of the nineteenth century and the civil rights movement of the twentieth. As the moral dimension of the environmental crisis becomes ever more apparent, we have reason to believe that religions will energize and support a new generation of leaders in the environmental movement. Religions have developed ethics for homicide, suicide, and genocide; now they are challenged to respond to biocide and ecocide.

The environmental crisis presents itself as the catalyst pressing individual religious traditions to awaken to their ecological role. In addition, it calls the religious traditions to cooperate in robust interreligious dialogue. Building on the efforts that have been made over the past several decades in ecumenical and interreligious circles, the religions may be able to transcend their differences for the good of a larger whole. The common ground for all humanity is the Earth itself and a shared sense of the interdependence of all life.

Religions Go Green

As scholars and theologians explore environmental ethics, religions are starting to find their voices regarding the environment. The monotheistic traditions of Judaism, Christianity, and

Islam are formulating original eco-theologies and eco-justice practices for stewardship and care for creation. Hinduism and Jainism in South Asia, and Buddhism in both Asia and the West, have undertaken projects of ecological restoration. Indigenous peoples bring to the discussion alternative ways of knowing and engaging the natural world. All those religious traditions are moving forward to find the language, symbols, rituals, and ethics for encouraging protection of bioregions and species. Religions are beginning to generate the energy needed for restoring the Earth by such practices as tree planting, coral-reef preservation, and river cleanup.

Some of the most striking examples of the intersection of religion and ecology have taken place in Iran and Indonesia. In June 2001 and May 2005, under former president Moham-mad Khatami, the government of Iran and the United Nations Environment Programme sponsored conferences in Tehran that focused on Islamic principles and practices for environ-mental protection. The Iranian Constitution identifies Islamic values that call for appropriate ecological practices and threatens legal sanctions against those who do not follow such practices. In Indonesia, projects of tree planting and restora-tion draw on the Islamic principle of maintaining balance (*mizaan*) in nature. Students in Islamic boarding schools are taught such principles and are encouraged to apply the Islamic doctrine of trusteeship to their relationships with the environment.

In the United States, the greening of churches and synagogues has led religious communities to search out sustainable building materials and renewable energy sources through Interfaith Power and Light. A group of Christian leaders in the Evangelical Climate Initiative is focusing on climate change as a moral issue that will disproportionately hurt the poor around the world. The National Religious Partnership for the Environment has been working with Jewish and Christian organizations to promote environmental concern. The Green Yoga Association is exploring ways in which yoga practitioners can bring their meditative focus to greater awareness of environmental concern. The Green Nuns, a group of Roman Catholic religious women in North America, sponsors a variety of environmental programs drawing on the ecological vision of Thomas Berry and Brian Swimme, who describe the story of the universe in both sacred and scientific terms. In Canada the Indigenous Environmental Network is speaking out about the negative effects of resource extraction and military-related pollution on First Nations Reserves. Internationally, the Greek Orthodox Ecumenical Patriarch Bartholomew has led several international symposia on religion, science, and the environment, focused primarily on water issues.

And finally, a conviction is emerging in some quarters that we need a new "species identity" to rally humanity to a stronger sense of solidarity than nationhood, faith, or family can muster. It means coming to understand our place within this vast field of force we call nature and evolutionary history. It means embracing a new story, a universe story, one that evokes awe, wonder, and responsibility and inspires humans to influence evolution in benign directions. "The time of innocence . . . is now past," declares Mihaly Csikszentmihalyi in his 1992 book *The Evolving Self*.

> It is no longer possible for mankind to blunder about self-indulgently. Our species has become too powerful to be led by instincts alone. Birds and lemmings cannot do much damage except to themselves, whereas we can destroy the entire matrix of life on the planet. The awesome powers we have stumbled into require a commensurate responsibility. As we become aware of the motives that shape our actions, as our place in the chain of evolution becomes clearer, we must find a meaningful and binding plan that will protect us and the rest of life from the consequences of what we have wrought.

With an awakening sense of global responsibility comes an emerging global ethics, such as that contained in the Earth Charter.

The Earth Charter, a document of enormous potential, emerged out of the United Nations Conference on Environment and Development (the Earth Summit) held in Rio de Janeiro in 1992. The international community, under the auspices of the United Nations, was seeking principles for guiding sustainable development. The Earth Charter is such a document, outlining the complex interdependency of humans and nature. It reflects the aspirations of the thousands of groups and individuals who helped to shape this people's document in the decade that followed the Earth Summit. It embodies the idea that the physical, chemical, and biological conditions for life delicately interact over time to bring forth and sustain life. Our response to this awesome interplay should be a sense of responsibility for its continuity. The Charter provides an integrated vision of three related areas for a viable future: ecological integrity; social and economic justice; and democracy, nonviolence, and peace. Care for the whole community of life is embraced by this declaration of interdependence (www.earthcharter.org).

A many-faceted alliance of religion and ecology, along with a new global ethics, is arising around the planet. Attitudes are being reexamined with alertness to the future of the whole community of life, not just of humans. This is a new moment for the world's religions, and they have a vital role to play in the emergence of a more comprehensive environmental ethics. The urgency cannot be underestimated. Indeed, the flourishing of the Earth community may depend on it.

Mary Evelyn Tucker is founder, with John Grim, of the Forum on Religion and Ecology (www.yale.edu/religionandecology). She is on the faculty of Yale University with joint appointments in the Divinity School, the School of Forestry and Environmental Studies, and the Department of Religious Studies as

Research Scholar and as Senior Lecturer in Religion and the Environment, respectively. Together with Grim she organized a series of conferences at Harvard on World Religions and Ecology and was series editor for ten volumes that emerged from it. Tucker has also written Worldly Wonder: Religions Enter Their Ecological Phase.

The Orthodox Church and the Environmental Crisis

Spiritual Insights and Personal Reflections

Patriarch Bartholomew

Protecting the natural environment has been at the top of our pastoral concern and agenda for at least the last two decades. The Ecumenical Patriarchate believes that the burning issue of the environment must be addressed at its root. And the root of this problem is the root of so many other problems: humanity. The problem lies in the choices we make on a daily basis in our personal lives, whether as individuals, as societies, or as nations. Human beings exploit their identity as the only rational beings and externalize their selfish attitudes, thereby inflicting significant and irrevocable damage on nature. The plain truth is that we are given the opportunity to enjoy and use God's creation, but instead we have chosen to exploit and abuse it.

As the first bishop of the Orthodox Christian Church worldwide, we have assumed the responsibility to sound the alarm. We feel that we must work and walk with all those persons who see the great risk and contribute to the restraint of this evil. Moreover, we must contribute as a church by raising the awareness and awakening the conscience of all who remain indifferent. We are certain that, when humanity as a whole becomes truly conscious that its very existence and survival depend on the environment, then the ecological problem will diminish, if not disappear. However, the world must be mobilized; and this mobilization must occur with a sense of critical urgency. Appropriate measures must be taken in timely fashion, because humankind has already delayed. Should we delay still further, then the dangers for all of us will become greater, and we shall no longer be able to turn around or hold back the current of events.

At the same time, we are obliged to recognize that we cannot expect to save the natural environment with the same methodology or "philosophy" concerning nature with which we have destroyed it. The sad reality is that many of us, especially in more affluent Western societies, have become accustomed to lifestyles of waste and greed. We are not always willing to undergo the sacrifice required of us in order to respond to the ecological crisis, and so we prefer either to ignore it deliberately or dismiss it indifferently. What we need is another, different worldview, a fresh perception of matter and the world. And the Ecumenical Patriarchate is convinced that, in this discernment of a new perception and meaning, religious traditions have an active role to play, and the Orthodox Church has a unique contribution to make.

The Role of Religious Communities

Churches and faith communities can be powerful allies in the struggle to prevent environmental degradation. Yet these institutions are sometimes the slowest to convince and the hardest to change, inasmuch as they are entrenched in ancient traditions, which over time have neglected the innate and intimate connection between humanity and nature.

The truth is that there is a binding unity and continuity that we share with all of God's creation. In recent years, we have been reminded of this truth by flora and fauna extinctions, by soil and forest losses, and by noise, air, and water pollution. Concern for the environment is not merely an emotional expression of superficial or sentimental love. It is a way of honoring and dignifying our creation by the hand and word of God. It is a way of listening to "the groaning of creation" (Romans 8:22).

We have been alienated from the natural world by the way we live and the priorities we pursue; at the same time, we have theologized and worshipped in a way that "spiritualizes" or "dematerializes" nature. As a result, the natural world is no longer associated with the meaning of life, our sense of the sacred, and the wonder of creation. Yet theology and liturgy are vital; indeed, they are profoundly related to our world and the natural environment. Of course, if we are to understand this, our ecological prayer must gradually move from the distant periphery of abstract theology or religious institutionalism to the center stage of our practical spirituality and pastoral ministry. In brief, our theology and spirituality must once again assume flesh; they must become "incarnate." They must be closely connected to our fellow human beings and to the natural environment.

Thus, as religious communities gradually awaken to the wisdom of their traditional beliefs, they will also begin to recognize that the environment is not only a political or a technological issue. For it is, in fact, primarily a religious and spiritual issue. Any form of religiosity or spirituality that remains disconnected from outward creation is ultimately also uninvolved with the inward mystery of all things.

The Environment and Liturgy

We tend to call this crisis an "ecological" crisis, which is a fair description insofar as its results are manifested in the ecological sphere. The message is clear: our way of life is humanly and environmentally suicidal. Unless we change it drastically, we cannot hope to avoid or reverse cosmic catastrophe. Yet the crisis is not first of all ecological. It is a crisis in the way we perceive reality and relate to our world. And the Orthodox liturgy offers a refreshing, alternative way of seeing ourselves in relation to the natural world.

A liturgical worldview signifies that everything that lives is holy, that everything that breathes praises God (Psalms 150:6), that the entire world is a "burning bush of God's energies," as Saint Maximus the Confessor put it in the seventh century. It also elicits a sacred response before the gift of creation, which we are called to return in thanksgiving to God as a gift for future generations. The same great theologian and saint of the early church also observed that "we should wage war not against the natural world, which has been created by God, but against those movements and energies of the essential powers within each of us that are disordered and unnatural and hostile to the natural world."

This is precisely the liturgical worldview preserved in the Orthodox Church, which proclaims a world imbued by God and a God involved in this world. Our original sin, so it seems, lies in our prideful refusal to receive the world as a gift of reconciliation, in our unwillingness humbly to regard the world as a sacrament of Communion. So at a time when we have polluted the air we breathe and the water we drink, we are called to restore within ourselves the sense of awe and delight, to respond to matter as to a mystery of ever-increasing connections. Such is the powerful message of the liturgy. And if we are guilty of relentless waste, it is perhaps because we have lost the spirit of worship. We are no longer respectful pilgrims on this Earth; we have been reduced to mere consumers.

The Ascetic Ethos

Responding to the environmental crisis is a matter of truthfulness to God, humanity, and the created order. It is not too far-fetched to speak of environmental damage as being a contemporary heresy or natural terrorism. We have repeatedly condemned this behavior as nothing less than sinful. For human beings to cause species to become extinct and to destroy the biological diversity of God's creation; for humans to degrade the integrity of the Earth by causing changes in its climate, by stripping the Earth of its natural forests, or by destroying its wetlands; for humans to injure other humans with disease by contaminating the Earth's waters, its land, its air, and its life with poisonous substances—all these are sins before God, humanity, and the world. We have tended to restrict the notion of sin to the individual sense of guilt or the social sense of wrongdoing. Yet sin also contains a cosmic dimension, and repentance from environmental sin demands a radical transformation of the way we perceive the natural world and a tangible change in the way we choose to live.

In short, the Orthodox Church speaks of an ascetic ethos that is required of all people. Admittedly, asceticism carries with it the baggage of dualism and denial, developed over many centuries. Yet Orthodox spirituality understands the notion of asceticism differently, as a vision of wholeness. For the ascetic discipline reminds us of the reality of human failure and the need for cosmic repentance. What is required from us is nothing less than an honest reflection on, and a radical reversal of, our attitudes and practices. There is a price to pay for our wasting the Earth's resources. This is what is meant by the cost of self-discipline. The solution to our ecological impasse lies in the denial of selfishness and self-centeredness. This spirit of asceticism leads to a sense of gratitude and the rediscovery of beauty.

The ascetic way is ultimately a way of liberation, and the ascetic is the one who is free, uncontrolled by attitudes that abuse the world, uncompelled by ways that use the world, and characterized by self-control and by the ability to say "no" or "enough." The ascetic way is moving away from what we want as individuals to what the world as a whole needs. It is valuing everything for itself, and not simply for ourselves. It is regaining a sense of wonder and being filled with a sense of goodness. Therefore, the ascetic dimension is the necessary corrective for our culture of wasting. It teaches us to share and not simply to consume.

We All Are Responsible

Behind the ecological problem, as behind many other contemporary issues, there lies concealed a theological stance and attitude. Western society's alienation from God, neighbor, and natural environment, as well as its emphasis on individualism and utilitarianism, has undoubtedly led to the abuse of sacred creation and to our modern ecological impasse. Humanity has lost the liturgical relationship between the Creator God and the creation; instead of serving as priests and stewards, human beings have been reduced to tyrants and abusers of nature.

Of course, we religious people are not political leaders, whose task is to propose or impose solutions. Yet we are obliged in the name of our faith and of truth to proclaim the need to change people's lifestyles and attitudes, to preach what is called in spiritual terms *metanoia* (or repentance), which implies justice and compassion. The lack of a sense of justice leads to greed and exploitation of the weaker by the more powerful, an abundance of wealth for the strong, and extreme poverty for the weak. Similarly, the lack of a spirit of compassion renders the soul indifferent to other people's pain and insensible to those things that kindle a sense of justice.

Therefore, we must broaden our notion of the environment to include the human and cultural environment. It would be a paradox to be concerned solely for the Earth while lacking interest in and concern for humanity and our cultural heritage. Just as the natural environment deserves our respect and protection, the human environment also deserves our attention and love. It is crucial that we recognize and respond to the interdependence between caring for the poor and caring for the Earth. They are two sides of the same coin. Indeed, the way we treat those who are suffering is directly reflected in the way we approach the ecological crisis. And both in turn mirror the way we perceive the divine mystery in all people and things— the way we kneel in prayer before the living God.

*His All Holiness, **Bartholomew**, Archbishop of Constantinople, New Rome, and Ecumenical Patriarch, is the 270th successor of the two-thousand-year-old local Christian church founded by Saint Andrew. Patriarch Bartholomew plays vital roles as the primary spiritual leader of the Orthodox Christian world and a transnational figure of global significance. As Ecumenical Patriarch he transcends every national and ethnic group on a global level and today is the spiritual leader of approximately 250 million faithful worldwide. As a citizen of Turkey, he has a unique perspective on the continuing dialogue among the Christian, Islamic, and Jewish worlds. Among his many leadership efforts in this realm is his cosponsorship, in 1994 and 2005, of the Peace and Tolerance Conference in Istanbul, which brought together Christians, Muslims, and Jews.*

Also notable is his work in promoting environmental awareness, which has earned him the title "Green Patriarch." He has cosponsored environmental seminars with His Royal Highness Prince Philip and organized international symposia on religion, science, and the environment at locations around the world, the most recent taking place on the coast of Greenland and centering on the issue of global warming. These endeavors, together with his inspiring efforts on behalf of religious freedom and human rights, rank Ecumenical Patriarch Bartholomew among the world's foremost apostles of love, peace, and reconciliation for humanity, for which he was awarded the Congressional Gold Medal.

Heaven and Earth Meet

from "Homily on the Occasion of the 2007
Christmas Eve Midnight Mass"

Pope Benedict XVI

The message of Christmas makes us recognize the darkness of a closed world, and thereby no doubt illustrates a reality that we see daily. Yet it also tells us that God does not allow himself to be shut out. He finds a space, even if it means entering through the stable; there are people who see his light and pass it on. Through the word of the Gospel, the angel also speaks to us, and in the sacred liturgy the light of the Redeemer enters our lives. Whether we are shepherds or "wise men," the light and its message call us to set out, to leave the narrow circle of our desires and interests, to go out to meet the Lord and worship him. We worship him by opening the world to truth, to good, to Christ, to the service of those who are marginalized and in whom he awaits us. . . .

Gregory of Nyssa, in his Christmas homilies, developed the same vision, setting out from the Christmas message in the

Gospel of John: "He pitched his tent among us" (John 1:14). Gregory applies this passage about the tent to the tent of our body, which has become worn out and weak, exposed everywhere to pain and suffering. And he applies it to the whole universe, torn and disfigured by sin.

What would he say if he could see the state the world is in today, through the abuse of energy and its selfish and reckless exploitation? Anselm of Canterbury, in an almost prophetic way, once described a vision of what we witness today in a polluted world whose future is at risk: "Everything was as if dead, and had lost its dignity, having been made for the service of those who praise God. The elements of the world were oppressed, they had lost their splendor because of the abuse of those who enslaved them for their idols, for whom they had not been created" (*Patrologia Latina* 158, 955–56). Thus, according to Gregory's vision, the stable in the Christmas message represents the ill-treated world.

What Christ rebuilds is no ordinary palace. [This refers to a familiar interpretation of the Bethlehem stable as a "crumbling palace," the ruin of David's kingdom from which a new kind of kingdom is born.—Ed.] He came to restore beauty and dignity to creation, to the universe: this is what began at Christmas and makes the angels rejoice. The Earth is restored to good order by virtue of the fact that it is opened up to God, it obtains its true light anew, and in the harmony between human will and divine will, in the unification of height and depth, it regains its beauty and dignity. Thus Christmas is a feast of restored creation. It is in this context that the Fathers interpret the song of the angels on that holy night: it is an expression of joy over the fact that the height and the depth, Heaven and Earth, are once more united; that man is again united to God. According to the Fathers, part of the angels' Christmas song is the fact that now angels and men can sing together, and in this way the beauty of the universe is expressed in the beauty of the song of praise. Liturgical song—still according to the Fathers—possesses its own peculiar dignity through the fact that it is sung together with the celestial choirs. It is the encounter with Jesus Christ that makes us capable of hearing the song of the angels, thus creating the real music that fades away when we lose this singing-with and hearing-with.

In the stable at Bethlehem, Heaven and Earth meet. Heaven has come down to Earth. For this reason, a light shines from the stable for all times; for this reason joy is enkindled there; for this reason song is born there. At the end of our Christmas meditation, I should like to quote a remarkable passage from Saint Augustine. Interpreting the invocation in the Lord's Prayer, "Our Father who art in Heaven," he asks: what is this—Heaven? And where is Heaven? Then comes a surprising response: " . . . who art in Heaven—that means: in the saints and in the just. Yes, the heavens are the highest bodies in the universe, but they are still bodies, which cannot exist except in a given location. Yet if we believe that God is located in the heavens, meaning in the highest parts of the world, then the birds would be more fortunate than we, since they would live closer to God. Yet it is not written: 'The Lord is close to those who dwell on the heights or on the mountains,' but rather: 'the Lord is close to the brokenhearted' (Psalm 34:18 [33:19]), an expression that refers to humility. Just as the sinner is called 'Earth,' so by contrast the just man can be called 'Heaven' " (*Sermo in monte* II 5, 17).

Heaven does not belong to the geography of space, but to the geography of the heart. And the heart of God, during the holy night, stooped down to the stable: the humility of God is Heaven. And if we approach this humility, then we touch Heaven. Then the Earth too is made new. With the humility of the shepherds, let us set out, during this holy night, toward the Child in the stable! Let us touch God's humility, God's heart! Then his joy will touch us and will make the world more radiant. Amen.

Pope Benedict XVI, Cardinal Joseph Ratzinger, is the 265th and reigning pope and also holds the office of Bishop of Rome. Elected in April 2005, succeeding Pope John Paul II, he is the spiritual head of the Roman Catholic Church and sovereign of the Vatican city-state. Benedict XVI is a well-known Roman Catholic theologian and a prolific author, and had a distinguished career as a professor of theology at various German universities before being

appointed Archbishop of Munich and Freising and Cardinal by Pope Paul VI. At the time of his election as pope, he had been prefect of the Congregation for the Doctrine of the Faith and was dean of the College of Cardinals.

Benedict XVI has made ecumenical overtures to most of the world's major faiths, and his support of environmental protection led Newsweek to call him the "green pope" upon his visit to New York in April 2008. The pontiff has called attention to environmental issues in his teachings and policy-making and called on Catholics to be better stewards of God's creation. In 2007 the Vatican became the world's only sovereign state to declare itself carbon-neutral, meaning that all its greenhouse gas emissions are offset through renewable energies and carbon credits. Among other efforts supported by His Holiness, solar panels to generate electricity were installed on the Vatican's historic buildings.

A Limitless Reality

from "The Burden of the Gospels"

Wendell Berry

The Gospels, like all other written works, impose on their readers the burden of their incompleteness. However partial we may be to the doctrine of the true account, or "realism," we must concede at last that reality is inconceivably great and any representation of it necessarily incomplete.

St. John at the end of his Gospel, remembering perhaps the third verse of his first chapter, makes a charming acknowledgement of this necessary incompleteness: "And there are also many other things which Jesus did, the which, if they should be written every one, I suppose that even the world itself could not contain the books that should be written." Our darkness, then, is not going to be completely lighted. Our ignorance finally is irremediable. We humans are never going to know everything, even assuming we have the capacity, because for reasons of the most insistent practicality we can't be told everything. We need to remember here Jesus's repeated admonitions to his disciples: You don't know; you don't understand; you've got it wrong.

The Gospels, then, stand at the opening of a mystery in which our lives are deeply, dangerously, and inescapably involved. This is a mystery that the Gospels can only partially reveal, for it could be fully revealed only by more books than the world could contain. It is a mystery that we are condemned but also are highly privileged to live our way into, trusting properly that to our little knowledge greater knowledge may be revealed. It is this privilege that should make us wary of any attempt to reduce faith to a rigmarole of judgments and explanations, or to any sort of familiar talk about God. Reductive religion is just as objectionable as reductive science, and for the same reason: Reality is large, and our minds are small.

And so the issue of reality—What is the *scope* of reality? What is real?—emerges as the crisis of this discussion. Right at the heart of the religious impulse there seems to be a certain solicitude for reality: the fear of foreclosing it or of reducing it to some merely human estimate. Many of us are still refusing to trust Caesar, in any of his modern incarnations, with the power to define reality. Many of us are still refusing to entrust that power to science. As inhabitants of the modern world, we are religious now perhaps to the extent of our desire to crack open the coffin of materialism, and to give to reality a larger, freer definition than is allowed by the militant materialists of the corporate economy and their political servants, or by the mechanical paradigm of reductive science. Or perhaps I can make most plain what I'm trying to get at if I say that many of us are still withholding credence, just as properly and for the same reasons, from any person or institution claiming to have the definitive word on the purposes and the mind of God.

It seems to me that all the religions I know anything about emerge from an instinct to push against any merely human constraints on reality. In the Bible such constraints are conventionally attributed to "the world" in the pejorative sense of that term, which we may define as the world of the creation *reduced* by any of the purposes of selfishness. The contrary purpose, the purpose of freedom, is stated by Jesus in the fourth Gospel: "I am come that they might have life, and that they might have it more abundantly."

This astonishing statement can be thought about and understood endlessly, for it is endlessly meaningful, but I don't think it calls for much in the way of interpretation. It does call for a very strict and careful reading of the word "life."

To talk about or to desire more abundance of anything has probably always been dangerous, but it seems particularly dangerous now. In an age of materialist science, economics, art, and politics, we ought not to be much shocked by the appearance of materialist religion. We know we don't have to look far to find people who equate more abundant life with a bigger car, a bigger house, a bigger bank account, and a bigger church. They are wrong, of course. If Jesus meant only that we should have more possessions or even more "life expectancy," then John 10:10 is no more remarkable than an advertisement for any commodity whatever. Abundance, in this verse, cannot refer to an abundance of material possessions, for life does not require a material abundance; it requires only a material sufficiency. That sufficiency granted, life itself, which is a membership in the living world, is already an abundance.

But even life in this generous sense of membership in creation does not protect us, as we know, from the dangers of avarice, of selfishness, of the wrong kind of abundance. Those dangers can be overcome only by the realization that in speaking of more abundant life, Jesus is not proposing to free *us* by making us richer; he is proposing to set *life* free from precisely that sort of error. He is talking about life, which is only incidentally our life, as a limitless reality.

Now that I have come out against materialism, I fear that I will be expected to say something in favor of spirituality. But if I am going to go on in the direction of what Jesus meant by "life" and "more abundantly," then I have got to avoid that duality of matter and spirit at all costs.

As every reader knows, the Gospels are overwhelmingly concerned with the conduct of human life, of life in the human commonwealth. In the Sermon on the Mount and in other places, Jesus is asking his followers to see that the way to more abundant life is the way of love. We are to love one another, and this love is to be more comprehensive than our love for family and friends and tribe and nation. We are to love our neighbors though they may be strangers to us. We are to love our enemies. And this is to be a practical love; it is to be practiced, here and now. Love evidently is not just a feeling but is indistinguishable from the willingness to help, to be useful to one another. The way of love is indistinguishable, moreover, from the way of freedom. We don't need much imagination to imagine that to be free of hatred, of enmity, of the endless and hopeless effort to oppose violence with violence, would be to have life more abundantly. To be free of indifference would be to have life more abundantly. To be free of the insane rationalizations for our desire to kill one another—that surely would be to have life more abundantly.

And where more than in the Gospels' teaching about love do we see that famously estranged pair, matter and spirit, melt and flow together? There was a Samaritan who came upon one of his enemies, a Jew, lying wounded beside the road. And the Samaritan had compassion on the Jew and bound up his wounds and took care of him. Was this help spiritual or material? Was the Samaritan's compassion earthly or heavenly? If those questions confuse us, that is only because we have for so long allowed ourselves to believe, as if to divide reality impartially between science and religion, that material life and spiritual life, earthly life and heavenly life, are two different things.

To get unconfused, let us go to a further and even more interesting question about the parable of the Samaritan: Why? Why did the Samaritan reach out in love to his enemy, a Jew, who happened also to be his neighbor? Why was the unbounding of this love so important to Jesus?

We might reasonably answer, remembering Genesis 1:27, that all humans, friends and enemies alike, have the same dignity, deserve the same respect, and are worthy of the same compassion because they are, all alike, made in God's image. That is enough of a mystery, and it implies enough obligation, to waylay us a while. It is certainly something we need to bear anxiously in mind. But it is also too human-centered, too potentially egotistical, to leave alone.

I think Jesus recommended the Samaritan's loving-kindness, what certain older writers called "holy living," simply as a matter of propriety, for the Samaritan was living in what Jesus understood to be a holy world. The foreground of the Gospels is occupied by human beings and the issues of their connection to one another and to God. But there is a background, and the background more often than not is the world in the best sense of the word, the world as made, approved, loved, sustained, and finally to be redeemed by God. Much of the action and the talk of the Gospels takes place outdoors: on mountainsides, lakeshores, riverbanks, in fields and pastures, places populated not only by humans but by animals and plants, both domestic and wild. And these nonhuman creatures, sheep and lilies and birds, are always represented as worthy of, or as flourishing within, the love and the care of God.

To know what to make of this, we need to look back to the Old Testament, to Genesis, to the Psalms, to the preoccupation with the relation of the Israelites to their land that runs through the whole lineage of the prophets. Through all this, much is implied or taken for granted. In only two places that I remember is the always implicit relation—the practical or working relation—of God to the creation plainly stated. Psalm 104:30, addressing God and speaking of the creatures, says, "Thou sendest forth thy spirit, they are created. . . ." And, as if in response, Elihu says to Job (34:14–15) that if God "gather unto himself his spirit and his breath; /All flesh shall perish together. . . ." I have cut Elihu's sentence a little short so as to leave the emphasis on the phrase "all flesh."

Those also are verses that don't require interpretation, but I want to stretch them out in paraphrase just to make as plain as possible my reason for quoting them. They are saying that not just humans but *all* creatures live by participating in the life of God, by partaking of his spirit and breathing his breath.* And so the Samaritan reaches out in love to help his enemy, breaking all the customary boundaries, because he has clearly seen in his enemy

* We now know that this relationship is even more complex, more utterly inclusive and whole, than the biblical writers suspected. Some scientists would insist that the conventional priority given to living creatures over the nonliving is misleading. Try, for example, to separate life from the lifeless minerals on which it depends.

not only a neighbor, not only a fellow human or a fellow creature, but a fellow sharer in the life of God.

When Jesus speaks of having life more abundantly, this, I think, is the life he means: a life that is not reducible by division, category, or degree, but is one thing, heavenly and earthly, spiritual and material, divided only insofar as it is embodied in distinct creatures. He is talking about a finite world that is infinitely holy, a world of time that is filled with life that is eternal. His offer of more abundant life, then, is not an invitation to declare ourselves as certified "Christians," but rather to become conscious, consenting, and responsible participants in the one great life, a fulfillment hardly institutional at all.

To be convinced of the sanctity of the world, and to be mindful of a human vocation to responsible membership in such a world, must always have been a burden. But it is a burden that falls with greatest weight on us humans of the industrial age who have been and are, by any measure, the humans most guilty of desecrating the world and of destroying creation. And we ought to be a little terrified to realize that, for the most part and at least for the time being, we are helplessly guilty. It seems as though industrial humanity has brought about phase two of original sin. We all are now complicit in the murder of creation. We certainly do know how to apply better measures to our conduct and our work. We know how to do far better than we are doing. But we don't know how to extricate ourselves from our complicity very surely or very soon.

How could we live without degrading our soils, slaughtering our forests, polluting our streams, poisoning the air and the rain? How could we live without the ozone hole and the hypoxic zones? How could we live without endangering species, including our own? How could we live without the war economy and the holocaust of the fossil fuels? To the offer of more abundant life, we have chosen to respond with the economics of extinction.

If we take the Gospels seriously, we are left, in our dire predicament, facing an utterly humbling question: How must we live and work so as not to be estranged from God's presence in His work and in all His creatures? The answer, we may say, is given in Jesus's teaching about love. But that answer raises another question that plunges us into the abyss of our ignorance, which is both human and peculiarly modern: How are we to make of that love an economic practice?

That question calls for many answers, and we don't know most of them. It is a question that those humans who want to answer will be living and working with for a long time—if they are allowed a long time. Meanwhile, may Heaven guard us from those who think they already have the answers.

Wendell Berry is the author of more than forty books of poetry, fiction, and essays, including his seminal work The Unsettling of America, *published by Sierra Club Books. He has been honored with the T. S. Eliot Award, the*

Aiken Taylor Award for poetry, and the John Hay Award of the Orion Society. Berry, together with his wife, Tanya, has farmed a hillside in his native Henry County, Kentucky, for more than forty years. They attend worship at Port Royal Baptist Church. This essay is adapted from a speech given in Lexington, Kentucky, in August 2005, at the first joint convocation of the Lexington Theological Seminary and the Baptist Seminary.

The Community of Creation

Sally Bingham

I belong to the community of life, and so do you. For the faithful and devout, this belonging is felt as a sense of communion with all of God's glorious creation. This sense brings with it a responsibility similar to that required in a healthy relationship of any kind. Each party has a role to play. If we are to have a balanced relationship with creation, we must recognize our dependence on a healthy world and, in turn, our role in caring for it. Care of creation is a responsibility of being human.

We who call ourselves Earth's stewards can go even further, to say that we belong to the community of creation—a phrase that embraces everything God created: every species, human and nonhuman, every living organism in the air or under the water or buried in the dirt. When I encountered the idea of creation as one massive living organism, it made sense to call it "community." This community is so intertwined and interconnected that, if one part is destroyed, the other parts will be affected.

It was this inner sense of communion with all of life that led me to wonder why clergy never spoke from the pulpit about protecting creation. We prayed for a "reverence for the earth" (*Book of Common Prayer*, 811), and in our baptismal vows we denounced "any evil that destroys the creatures of God." But curiously we never made the connection between those prayers and our behavior.

Throughout a ten-year period of college, seminary, and volunteer ministry, I struggled to understand why this was. Then I was ordained to the Episcopal priesthood and given the opportunity to preach about what I believe is the most important moral issue of our time: climate change. The warming trend now in progress is the greatest threat the community of creation has ever faced. Its human impact will be felt first by the poor, who contribute the least to the problem, but eventually everyone will be affected, human and nonhuman alike. Life in balance, as God provided and as we know it, will disappear.

I soon discovered, however, that it wasn't enough simply to preach about this profound threat. I had to act. I decided to engage in a religious response to global warming, and the organization called Interfaith Power and Light (IPL) was born, along with a campaign that I hope will help change the destructive course we have embarked on. IPL's mission is both practical—to lower the energy consumption of church buildings and religious organizations—and visionary: to help people of faith think and behave differently toward creation and one another. We must lead by example, which historically has been the role of religion.

In the hope of persuading others that such action can truly make a difference, I'll share some of the history of our work. IPL's predecessor was Episcopal Power and Light, which was created in 1997 when the electrical industry deregulated and California and Massachusetts became the first states to invite in "green marketers." The deregulated marketplace offered an opportunity to raise consciousness about energy sources, pollution, and global warming. We decided to ask churches to switch to clean, green power because it was the right and moral thing to do.

It was tough at the beginning, because green power was a hard sell: it was "new." People thought they would have to replace all the wiring in their churches in order to buy electricity from a source other than their known and trusted utility. I visited churches and made impassioned pleas to congregations to switch to clean power, assuring them that it would be easier than they thought. I made many presentations at educational classes between services. I gave fire-and-brimstone sermons on the sin of putting dirty, coal-burning power plants in poor neighborhoods and the injustices this brought, including high rates of lung disease and cancers among people too burdened with survival to do anything about it. Any parish that bought power from a dirty power plant was participating in this unjust system, I declared, reminding churchgoers that Jesus said, "What you do to the least of us, you do to me." Furthermore, the commandment "Love your neighbor as yourself" was *not* being followed if we continued polluting the air of poor neighborhoods.

It was clear to me that climate change was and is a social justice issue, one in which faith communities should take a leadership role, but at the time not many followed this line of thinking. My preaching mostly fell on deaf ears that first year. Then one day, Saint Aidan's Episcopal Church in San Francisco became the first church to switch to 100 percent wind energy. Their lights didn't go out, and they didn't have to move wires. Better still, they began to save money, because they installed compact fluorescent lightbulbs to offset the extra cost of getting power from green sources, producing a net savings. The news got out, and by the year 2000, sixty Episcopal churches in the state of California were buying some form of green electricity. We were saving money, we were creating jobs through the development of green technology, and we were on our way to saving creation.

Then in 2001, the "energy crisis" hit California. A combination of things brought it about: deregulation laws allowed the wholesale price to increase with no cap, but the retail price was limited, so utilities had to "buy high" and "sell low," without passing on the cost difference to consumers. Looking back, it seems that there was also some price manipulation by

Enron Corporation. In any case, the result was that the renewable-energy companies left California. Our model churches no longer had the green option and were switched back to "brown" power without any say in the matter. The green electricity trend was halted, for the moment.

Undaunted, we moved ahead with our message of renewable energy and conservation through a partnership formed in 2000 with the California Council of Churches. This gave us an expanded mailing list and access to the interfaith community. In a very short time, our audience grew a hundredfold, and we were talking to legislators about increasing the amount of renewable energy in the California grid. That share has been growing ever since, to the benefit of many. The partnership also was our entry into the world of advocacy. Meanwhile, under the new name California Interfaith Power and Light, we actively sought out congregations who would join us, cut their own carbon emissions, and serve as examples to the community.

In 2001, we hired a national campaign manager and took the California program across the country. Today the Interfaith Power and Light Campaign is active in twenty-eight states and more than five thousand congregations, representing all the mainstream religious traditions. We preach and teach the "good news" of energy conservation, efficiency, renewables, and how these connect to one's faith and responsibility to be a steward of creation.

Religion is finding its place in the environmental movement, and none too soon. Through our brief history, IPL has witnessed an enormous and encouraging shift in how people of faith are responding to this call. In attitude and scope, it's no less impressive than the (almost overnight) phenomenon of leaving cigarette smoking behind. Besides hearing the doctors and scientists say that "smoking will kill you," people were feeling the pain of cancer within their own circle of family and friends. Similarly, our awareness of the warming climate and its devastating effects has reached a tipping point. Enough lives have been touched—through extraordinary heat waves, disrupted crop cycles, drought, fires, and increased severity of storms—that governments, legislators, corporations, big and small businesses, and millions of individuals across the globe are making changes that will help solve this most important moral problem. Events like Hurricane Katrina and the success of the film *An Inconvenient Truth* were also key to raising awareness.

Beyond all this, the voice of religion—so often the moral voice of society—is growing stronger on the subject. The values young people learn early in a religious community—those of loving each other and loving God's works—are being expressed as care for creation and love of one's neighbor. From African-American Baptist pulpits in Atlanta to the most conservative Protestant cathedrals and Muslim mosques, we hear the message about saving creation. And on the practical level, some Jewish temples and Buddhist communities have been in the forefront, installing solar panels on their roofs.

I write with a hopeful heart and lots of evidence that our movement will soon reach a goal unimaginable just a few years ago: a complete shift in how we humans view our place on the planet. Crisis can bring opportunities, and currently we have an opportunity like none other in history. It is a chance to awaken spiritually, to redefine what it means to be human, and to bring light into our souls. All this is possible as we come to see ourselves as part of the community of creation and find a new place in what the poet Mary Oliver calls "the family of things." As we evolve in this direction, we are opening ourselves to something bigger than ourselves. We can and will survive in the community of creation if we live as if we belong to it and love it.

The Reverend Canon Sally Bingham serves as canon for the environment at the Diocese of California in San Francisco. She founded the Regeneration Project, a nonprofit that created the national Interfaith Power and Light Campaign to unite all faiths in efforts to prevent the catastrophic effects of global warming. State chapters of Interfaith Power and Light work with congregations to help them reduce their carbon footprints and publicize the call to combat global warming. In 2006 the Regeneration Project brought together Muslim, Jewish, and Christian leaders for a summit about the reality of global warming and the imperative for a religious response. In 2007, Grist magazine named Bingham one of the world's most important green religious leaders, third on its list of fifteen, after the Dalai Lama and Ecumenical Patriarch Bartholomew.

Two Towns, Two Crosses

Cassandra Carmichael

Enter the boat channel from Chesapeake Bay to Tangier Island, Virginia, and it is there—a simple white wooden cross.

To reach the body of water that divides Maryland's Eastern Shore from Tangier, you drive down Route 50, flanked on both sides of the road by rows of corn and forests of trees. You won't see many waterways, but you'll sense the great expanses of marsh, creeks, and rivers that make up the Chesapeake Bay ecosystem lying just around the bend. If you leave the beach traffic of Route 50 to seek the quieter Routes 13 and 413, you'll eventually find your way to another way of life at the end of the road.

The city dock in Crisfield, Maryland, where the road dead-ends, is the gateway to a world of watermen and a few women who "farm" the bounty of Chesapeake Bay for crabs, oysters, and clams. ("Waterman" is an old English term referring to people who harvest more than one fishery: crab, oyster, or finned fish.) Life for professional watermen is challenging and physically demanding, but most wouldn't trade their way of life for any other. However, shellfish populations are dwindling because of poor water quality and shrinking habitat in the bay, caused by shoreline development, pollution from nearby cities, and agricultural runoff. Along with rising operating costs, this has gravely endangered the watermen's livelihood.

And nowhere is the pinch felt more keenly than on Tangier Island, an hour's boat ride from Crisfield. Living on an island with no connecting bridges, the seven hundred residents, who mostly work the waters for blue crabs, rely exclusively on the bay to support them. Perhaps this tenuous existence, subject to the vagaries of the bay, accounts for the deep-seated religious faith of this community. Most consider themselves conservative, evangelical Christians and attend one of the two churches on the island. Many watermen carry a placard of Christ on their boats as a reminder that they are protected and restored by their Christian faith. As one resident, Carlene Shores, says, "Nothing happens on Tangier unless it is rooted and grounded in the church."

In the 1990s, disputes erupted between the islanders and a local conservation group over crab regulations set by the state board of fisheries. The new regulations, which were influenced by proposals from conservation groups, were opposed by many Tangier watermen because they decreased the allowed catch. While the islanders have a healthy respect for the bay and recognize their reliance on its bounty, they have resisted what they see as interference from outsiders, such as state natural resource officials who are trying to protect the valuable blue crab populations. Arguments over fisheries have been part of the history of Chesapeake Bay for centuries. Back in the 1870s, oystermen would say, "Get it today! Hell with *tamar* [tomorrow]! Leave it till *tamar*, somebody else'll get it."

Susan Drake Emmerich, a researcher who came to Tangier to study the conflict, found herself performing a ministry of reconciliation, as she describes it. Over many months she met with both the islanders and the concerned environmentalists, pointing out the misunderstandings that had created mutual distrust.

A turning point came with a joint service for both church congregations on the island, which focused on the biblical basis for environmental stewardship. At that service, Emmerich talked about the image of Jesus as a pilot guiding the watermen, carried on many of boats. Should they put a blindfold on Jesus, she asked, so he wouldn't see them dumping trash into the bay waters or taking illegal crabs? "At that service," she writes, "fifty-eight watermen publicly committed to a Watermen's Stewardship Covenant, . . . to obeying all the laws as a result of obeying God's law, and to being better stewards of God's creation."

Emmerich's work led to the founding of the Tangier Watermen's Stewardship for the Chesapeake, an initiative based on a biblical understanding of the watermen's role as "caretakers" of God's creation. Led by Susan Parks and other Tangier natives, the effort has eased tensions and enabled islanders to more clearly see their role as God's faithful stewards in protecting the bay and the blue crab.

The results have been tangible. Watermen now practice good stewardship by properly disposing of oil and trash from their boats instead of throwing it overboard. And shoreline cleanups are regular events on the island. But most important, relations between local conservation groups and the watermen have improved.

Members of the Tangier Watermen's group speak of their work in ways that reveal their strong penchant for faith-based environmentalism. One of them, James (Ooker) Eskridge, is both a waterman and mayor of Tangier; he's also an active member of his church. When he isn't on the water, you'll often find him in his crab shanty, a building that sits on pilings above the water where he sorts and stores softshell crabs. It is hard for a visitor to not be awed and inspired by his sincere dedication to protecting the bay because it is what God's scripture instructs him to do. He recalls that, the day before the joint service, high tides brought heaps of trash up on the island, and people recognized that "their sins had washed ashore." He says, "The men who have taken the covenant are permanently changed. We can't go back. People have seen the light."

The people of this community, so dependent upon the water, have made strong connections between their faith and caring for God's creation, and it has put them in the religious spotlight. The National Council of Churches, recognizing the lessons that can be taught here, brings groups of young adults engaged in faith-based environmental work to the island every few years. The goal is to teach these professionals, in their twenties and thirties, about environmental and social justice issues, using the plight of the bay and the story of the Tangier waterman to demonstrate how profoundly the human world and the rest of God's creation are linked.

Drive through the bayou to the end of the road at Shell Beach, Louisiana, and it is there—an ornate metal cross.

To reach Shell Beach, home to a Louisiana shrimping community, you must leave the safety of the levee system that was built to protect residents of St. Bernard Parish from the waters of Lake Pontchartrain and the Mississippi River. Once you drive over the levee's earthen mound to the eastern side of St. Bernard Parish, you come into a world of wide-open wetlands and dwindling cypress swamps. The ride down the narrow, two-lane road to Shell Beach through the town of Yscloskey has changed over the years. The road, once canopied by massive cypresses, is now starkly guarded by a few lone trees, mostly stripped bare of limbs and leaves.

The cypress forests are diminishing because shipping channels for oil and gas companies have been cut into the precious wetlands, allowing salt water to infiltrate the delicate bayous. The

Mississippi River–Gulf Outlet Canal (MRGO), at seventy-six miles long, is the best known and most controversial of the shipping channels that provide shortened water travel from the Gulf of Mexico to the New Orleans harbor. These channels have helped change the ecology of the wetlands, salinating the water and creating phenomenal erosion that results in the loss of seventy-five square kilometers of wetlands every year. Because of erosion, the MRGO, originally designed to be 650 feet wide, now averages 1,500 feet in width.

The dwindling of cypress swamp and wetlands has implications not only for the bounty of the region's fisheries and for its other wildlife but also for the human communities such as Shell Beach and Yscloskey. Wetlands that once provided protection have lost their power to absorb ever-increasing storm surges. The consequences have been dire: engineers have implicated the MRGO canal in the increased storm surge and levee failure following Hurricane Katrina.

Katrina ripped through Louisiana's eastern bayous on August 29, 2005, bringing an eighteen-foot storm surge—high enough to knock entire houses off their foundations. The drive to Shell Beach, even years after the storm, still passes stone front-porch steps leading nowhere. As reported in a *National Geographic* story, Robert Guzman of Yscloskey lost his house to flooding, which he attributes in part to the destructive shipping channel. "The house is across the highway in the trees now," he reported shortly after Katrina. "About everything we owned is gone."

A small metal bridge in Yscloskey crosses over a narrow strip of shallow bayou where a historically productive shrimping fleet is tied up. With nets at the ready, the shrimpers that remain after Katrina are busy working on their boats, preparing for long hours spent on the water. Of the boat owners that were in Yscloskey and the surrounding communities when Katrina hit, many chose to let their boats ride out the storm in Violet Canal, located nearby, just inside the protective levee system. Even there, caught between a natural disaster and the human-made complication of disappearing wetlands, the fleet almost perished but for the tenacity of its crews. When the shrimpers returned home, they found little left of the community they knew and loved. A small ice plant, which had once provided them with an invaluable service, lies in tattered ruins, no longer in business.

Since Katrina, many residents have referred to the MRGO as "Hurricane Highway." The U.S. Army Corp of Engineers has announced plans to close the channel—though the move comes several years too late to prevent the devastation. Katrina still hangs heavy in the air as relief and rebuilding efforts proceed with painful slowness. Talk to residents and you'll hear concerns about the disappearing wetlands and the extreme hardships that came after Katrina. But you'll also find in this community a quiet faith, a uniquely Cajun sense of humor, and a fortitude that has enabled them to endure both the challenges of working the water and the aftermath of a deadly hurricane.

As in the wake of any disaster, the focus is on rebuilding homes and lives. With more than ninety thousand square miles in the Gulf region declared federal disaster areas, there has been much brokenness to mend. Churches throughout St. Bernard Parish—from Corinne Baptist in Violet, to Our Lady of Prompt Succor Catholic Church in Chalmette, to Amazing Grace Fellowship in Arabi—have risen to the occasion, providing material and spiritual aid as well as a place to socialize for hurricane victims, who often end up isolated.

As the second anniversary of Hurricane Katrina approached, the National Council of Churches brought a small group of clergy to Shell Beach to witness the rebuilding, as well as the fortitude of faith apparent in the residents. These clergy members heard firsthand how the people of the bayou—like the Tangier Islanders—are making connections between their beliefs and how society's failure to care for God's creation (in this case the protective wetlands) led to their plight. And like the young adult fellows who visited Tangier, the clergy visiting Shell Beach recognized the profound faith that guides the people of Shell Beach through any storm.

The congregation of Amazing Grace Fellowship lost its church building and about half its members, but they cling together while rebuilding membership and seeking a new home. Says the Reverend Rick Hager, who took over as pastor two months before Katrina, "When you feel like you've lost all hope, you find that you still have a little bit of faith left, and you keep moving forward."

In August 2006, a steel cross and stone monument known as the Shell Beach Memorial was dedicated to the 129 citizens of St. Bernard Parish lost to the storm.

Two towns. Separated by an expanse of land and a time zone. Both bearing the brunt of environmental and economic struggles. Both bearing a cross at the water's edge as a symbol of their faith and fortitude.

While the communities of Tangier Island and Shell Beach have distinctly different cultures, they share a common bond in depending on the water for their livelihoods. And both suffer from outside development pressures. The shrimpers of Shell Beach rely on the protection of the wetlands, which are being sacrificed to oil and gas interests. The watermen of Tangier rely for their crab harvests on the health of the Chesapeake Bay waters, which are being jeopardized by pollution runoff and residential development.

Yet for the people of these towns, the cross that stands at the mouth of each harbor represents a power greater than the threats they face. For Christians, that symbol speaks of the strength of faith, hope, resurrection, and love that can sustain them.

Cassandra Carmichael is director of the eco-justice program at the National Council of Churches, where she helps serve the environmental ministries of the council's thirty-five member denominations, which represent a hundred thousand churches nationwide. As a member of Calvary United Methodist Church in Annapolis, Maryland, she serves on the church's creation care committee and has helped with its greening projects, including increasing the stream buffer area on the church property.

Quotations from Tangier Islanders and background on this issue are from "Fostering Environmental Responsibility on the Part of the Watermen of Chesapeake Bay: A Faith and Action Research Approach" by Susan Drake Emmerich, in Christians Engaging Culture (Harold Heie and Michael King, eds.). Background on Shell Beach is partly based on reports in the New Orleans Times-Picayune.

Science, Scripture, and Con-serving Creation

Calvin B. DeWitt

Evening is approaching as I ponder the forest though my old office window. It has been a wondrously sunny day with bright sunlight reflected by pure white snow; now the scene darkens. My view on creation here is through a kind of porthole in Earth Hall—an earth-and-snow-sheltered refuge in which I am writing, beneath an eighteen-inch blanket of soil covered with an equally thick blanket of freshly fallen snow. My hibernal habitat, from whence I compose a message of hope as I have at this desk for a quarter century.

On this first day in February, graduate students from five universities have come to a snowy retreat here at Au Sable Institute to refresh themselves at the interface of their graduate scientific education and their Christian faith. I'm joining them and their mentors to help us stay on track—to help us work toward mutual understanding, respect, and cooperation across the divide that has come to separate faith and science, and to help these students enter fulfilling vocations of responsible service. I will share with them recent progress in bridging this divide: recent conversations with biologist E. O. Wilson on his "extending the olive branch" to evangelicals and on his 2006 book *The Creation*; and an extraordinary meeting of prominent scientists and evangelical leaders in Georgia in December 2007. Six weeks after meeting at Melhana Plantation, this group of scientists and evangelical leaders presented "An Urgent Call to Action" at the National Press Club in Washington, D.C.—during which we also announced the agreement among us to reinstate use of the phrase "the creation" in our scientific and religious vocabularies. This cooperation and good spirit across scientific and religious divides encouraged us all. Agreeing to be true to ourselves, to our science, and to our faith commitments, we agreed to work in concert to care for creation.

For me, this work is a beautiful extension or enlargement of the tapestry that began at my birth—a tapestry my community called our "world-and-life-view."

This world-and-life-view prompted me to love science and practice joyful stewardship—to care for creation. It began with keeping a turtle in a tub in our backyard. This was the beginning of a backyard zoo that steadily grew and developed and that, in my teens, extended to an aviary and aquarium my parents allowed me to build in our basement. My menagerie indoors and out was built in harmony with what I was learning in church on how best to live and respond to creation.

Each of us has our own peculiar beginning. This beginning for me included "two-books theology"—a perspective on the Bible and science that owes its origin to New Testament times. At the heart of this in my growing up was the great integrative statement of the Confession of Faith used for centuries by churches of the Reformed tradition. As printed on the back pages of the *Psalter Hymnal* of 1932, 1959, and 1988, the principal songbook of my life, its second article proclaimed,

> We know God by two means:
> First by the creation, preservation, and governance
> of the universe
> which is before our eyes as a most elegant book
> in which all creatures, great and small, are as letters
> leading us to see clearly the invisible things of God:
> his eternal power and divinity. . . .
> Second, he makes himself known more clearly and
> fully
> by his holy and divine word, as far as is necessary for
> us to know
> in this life, to his glory and our salvation.

I have built from this beginning over the decades, empowered by this "two-books" heritage, which also inspired many other scientists and field naturalists. I have learned from my study and research that the joy and discovery that comes from reading both books requires that they be read coherently—one must read *within* each and *between* the two. Such coherent reading fosters a conscious and deliberate world-and-life-view that seeks and finds a vocation of service to both science and faith. It fosters a loving care for creation that is rooted in science and guided by ethics.

What wonderful knowledge is to be gained by studying and beholding creatures—past and present, living and nonliving, great and small! Our textbooks, journal articles, and field guides contain but summaries of the teachings about the myriad of creatures (that is, the works of creation): from subatomic particles to galaxies; purple sulfur bacteria to blue whales. "Great are the works of the Lord;/They are studied by all who delight in them!" wells up in my mind and spirit! My heritage of psalm-singing is "uncorked," and out bursts the text of Psalm 111:2.

As this bright day turns to dusk, I ponder my place on this planet. From west to east, I look out to the Great Lakes Forest, while behind me is the east portal that funnels graduate fellows past walls of glacial rocks and cobbles into the warmth of the earth and snow that shelter us. Looking farther west, I can see in my mind's eye the reality of Yosemite—rock temples on this turning planet still bathed in glorious light. Behind me very far to the east, on Scotland's coast, night has fallen under tender light of moon and stars. Illuminating creation's text and brightening human spirits, there is light. Yosemite's still-bright light discloses the clear text of the "glacial scriptures." Scotland's softer light—the lunar, stellar, and auroral light of night—calls for a more tender reading of creation.

Creation's light was celebrated a century ago by another reader of the two books. Wrote John Muir at Alaska's Glacier Bay, "The white, rayless light of morning, seen when I was alone amid the peaks of the California Sierra, had always seemed to me the most telling of all the terrestrial manifestations of God." Muir and I share a common religious heritage, and so I felt great empathy as I walked the paths of Scotland's coast this past summer—paths at Dunbar where Johnnie Muir played, hiked, climbed, and learned from creation's book, even as he also learned his catechism, memorized most of the Bible, and sang from the Scottish Psalter.

Why are these things of our childhood and youth not simply set aside as we grow up? Why are they not forgotten, thereby allowing us to proceed unencumbered in our science and study of natural history? It is, I believe, because doxology necessarily breaks forth from a well of joy, a profound well from which joy continues to flow. It is an artesian gusher that cannot be suppressed as it wells up from its deep and inspired cultural roots. Scripture and psalms, coupled with two-books theology, is a well of joy, deep and profound. This heritage implants doxologies in heart and mind that break forth on every instance of discovery and disclosure of creation's wonders: "Praise God from Whom all blessings flow!" exclaims Muir time and again. "Praise God all creatures here below!"

In seeking the deep sources of such doxologies, I came to articulate four ethical principles informed both by science and theology. The first three are Earthkeeping, Fruitfulness, and Sabbath. Their capstone principle is Con-servancy. These four principles not only are discoverable in the Bible (and thus rooted in my heritage) but also are remarkably in accord with science—with the results of our scientific investigations of the biosphere and its creatures, including people. To bring you into the biblical texts I find to be wonderfully ecological, a good place to begin is the beginning: the book of Genesis.

The Earthkeeping Principle

A most important thing about Genesis is that it begins by professing a single cause, a single origin, of the universe, the planet, and the biosphere. Another is that everything created and brought forth is declared to be good. And still another is its insistence that neither the creation nor any of its creatures are gods. In bringing home this last point, Genesis avoids the godly name "Sun" by calling it "the greater light," and avoids the godly name "Moon" by naming it "the lesser light." These heavenly bodies and other material creatures are so nondivine that people are given dominion over them and even can put the kibosh on them.

This "dominion," however, clearly is not *domination*. Quite the contrary, it is *service*. Human beings are responsible to their Maker, not to Sun or Moon or any other "gods." The "human of the humus," the "earthling of the earth," "the Adam of *adamah*," we are told, is expected to *'avad* the garden and *shamar* it. The vocation of the human earthling is not to trash or destroy the creation or its creatures or otherwise dominate them, but to serve and safeguard them. The Hebrew word *'avad*, translated as "till," "dress," and "work" in some biblical versions, is translated as "serve" in Young's *Literal Translation of the Bible*. This "service word" charges the human earthlings to meet the needs of what is guarded—the "guarden" must be sustained so that it may flourish. They are to live their lives in joyful service, diligently safeguarding the guarden.

The Hebrew word for "keep" is *shamar*, as in: "The Lord bless you and *keep* you." This blessing does not ask that those blessed be kept in a kind of preserved, static, and uninteresting state, but that they be kept in dynamic integrity—with all their vitality, energy, and beauty. This keeping sustains supporting relationships with family, neighbors, and friends; with the land, air, and water of the Earth; and of course with the one whose love for them and the world they mirror. In Genesis, the word *shamar* has the same meaning for the garden and creation. It brings to the guarden and the biosphere a keeping that nurtures all their life-sustaining and life-fulfilling relationships.

It is a calling—a vocation—to *keep* the creation. "People of the Book"—Jewish, Christian, and Islamic men, women, and children—might summarize the Earthkeeping Principle this way: As God *keeps* us, so we should *keep* God's creation. The Earthkeeping Principle resonates well with our scientific understanding of ecosystems and the biosphere, and our understanding that human beings must strive to safeguard the ecological systems and ecosystem services that sustain all life on Earth.

The Fruitfulness Principle

It is also in Genesis that the great blessing of fruitfulness is given to all creation. "Let the waters teem with living creatures, and let birds fly above the earth across the vault of the sky" (1:20). "Be fruitful and increase in number and fill the water in the seas, and let the birds increase on the earth" (1:22). "Let the land produce living creatures according to their kinds, creatures that move along the ground, and wild animals, each according to its kind" (1:24).

This is amplified in "the great nature psalm," Psalm 104:

> He makes springs pour water into the ravines;
>   it flows between the mountains.
> They give water to all the beasts of the field;
>   the wild donkeys quench their thirst.
> The birds of the air nest by the waters;
>   they sing among the branches.
> He waters the mountains from his upper chambers;
>   the land is satisfied by the fruit of his work.

Another song, the "psalm of the good shepherd" (Psalm 23) describes the fruitful provisions of "green pastures" and "still waters" even as the Shepherd "restores our soul."

For me, the most exciting biblical passage on fruitfulness is about Noah and the ark. The Fruitfulness Principle includes safeguarding the long lineages of the living creatures of Earth. It expects us to enjoy creation and its many fruits, but requires that we not destroy the *fruitfulness* that sustains creation. Reinforcing this, the prophet Ezekiel proclaimed, "Is it not enough for you to feed on the good pasture? Must you also trample the rest of your pasture with your feet? Is it not enough for you to drink clear water? Must you also muddy the rest with your feet?" (Ezekiel 34:18). Conservationist Aldo Leopold was among the first modern ecologists to open up this passage. Speaking of land fruitfulness in his essay "The Forestry of the Prophets," he wrote, "Individual thinkers since the days of Ezekiel and Isaiah have asserted that the despoliation of land is not only inexpedient but wrong."

The Fruitfulness Principle accords with what we know scientifically about what maintains the abundance of life upon which the biosphere depends and what makes it flourish. Human beings must make sure that we safeguard the lineages of the plants and animals that live on Earth, and that we preserve and restore the fruitful services of ecosystems, for our well-being and that of all creation.

The Sabbath Principle

There is a biblical requirement to punctuate our lives with periods of rest. The Sabbath is given to help us all get off the treadmill, to protect us from the hazards of continuous work, to help us pull our lives together again. It's a time to worship, to enjoy the fruits of creation, to rest and restore ourselves and the animals under our care. It goes beyond people, however, to include the land. Nothing in creation must be relentlessly pressed. "For six years you are to sow your fields and harvest the crops, but during the seventh year let the land lie unplowed and unused. Then the poor among your people may get food from it, and the wild animals may eat what they leave. Do the same with your vineyard and your olive grove" (Exodus 23:10–11).

The power of this biblical principle became clear to me several years ago as I drove north from Edmonton to visit a Canadian farm family on the fifty-fourth parallel. As I neared their community, I was startled by a timber wolf crossing the road in front of me. When I arrived at my destination a few minutes later, I was even more startled by this family's answer to my anxious question, "Do you have timber wolves around here?" Their reply was an excited "Yes!" I soon found that this family treasured the wolf as God's creature, to be kept along with the rest of the land they held in trust. Equally startling was finding that they allowed their barley fields to lie fallow every second year, providing rest for the land. Their reason? "The Bible requires it."

But why did they let their land rest every *second* year, instead of every *seventh*? "You remember Christ's teaching about how the Sabbath of the week is made for people, and not the other way around? Well, the same is true for the land. The Sabbath is made for the land, and not the land for the Sabbath," said the farmer. Again I asked, " But why every *second* year?" "Because that is what the land needs," he replied. "With the limited rainfall and this high latitude, the land would become degraded if it were forced to produce more often." The Sabbath keeps and protects people, families, animals, and all creation from being relentlessly pressed.

The Con-servancy Principle

We must return creation's service to us with service of our own. This principle overarches all the others. The word *con-servancy* refers to conservation, often denoting an organization that regulates fisheries or protects sensitive natural areas. Earlier, when I discussed the Earthkeeping Principle, I noted from Genesis 2:15 that the human earthling was expected to *serve* the creation in addition to keeping it. The Hebrew word *'avad* (serve) is a word widely used in the Bible, occurring 290 times in the Old Testament.

We already know from experience with the "beautiful book" of creation that this garden serves us. It serves us with good food, beauty, herbs, fiber, medicine, pleasant microclimates, continual soil-making, nutrient processing, and seed production. The garden and the larger biosphere provide what ecologists call "ecosystem services," such as water purification by evaporation and percolation, moderation of flood peaks and drought flows by river-system wetlands, development of soils from the weathering of rocks, and moderation of local climates by nearby bodies of water. Yet Genesis addresses *our* service to the garden. The garden's service *to us* is implicit; service *by us* to the garden is explicit.

Like Adam, we are expected to return the service of the garden with service of our own. This is a reciprocal service, a "service with"—in other words, a *con-service*, a *con-servancy*, a *con-servation*. This reciprocal service defines an engaged relationship between garden and gardener, between the biosphere and its safeguarding stewards.

We can call this principle of "never taking from creation without returning service of our own" the Con-servancy Principle. Our love of our Creator God, God's love of creation, and our imaging this love of God—all join together to commission us as *con-servers* of creation. As con-servers, we follow the example of the second Adam—Jesus Christ (see I Corinthians 15:22, 45).

The forest outside my window now is black; the snow flowers, now unseen, are continuing to descend. No moonlight or aurora borealis this night, and so unseen they fall. No matter the compass direction of the winds, vapors from the moisture-laden air over the Great Lakes traverse the right distance for cooling, crystallizing, and precipitating—no matter whether from Lake Michigan on the west, the Straits of Mackinac on the north, or Lake Huron on the east. Images of the falling crystals' remarkable symmetry, endless variety, and magnificent beauty remain even as they turn to liquid, making us burst with wonder—even praise! Snow flowers keep falling—the duration of falling so great that snowshoes become necessary for traversing their accumulations, even as the skink hibernates beneath their insulating blanket and the snowshoe hare chews on tree branches brought within reach by the thickening blanket.

Thousands of miles west at higher altitudes, similar snow flowers are falling, some of which will persist over the years, forming glaciers that, after time lags great and small, will form meltwater that waters the Earth and its living creatures. The compressed snow flowers will turn to liquid to descend along waterways to the plains below, eventually to sweetly evaporate to misty heights again to descend as dew, snow, and rain.

Wind is whipping snow flowers into great drifts. The plow coming down the drive to our glacial drumlin pushes aside quadrillions of snow flowers and more, into the marsh on either side. Marvelous beauty, wonderful blessings, doxology! Coming from above, coming on the north wind, blanketing the landscape, insulating the marsh.

It now is more necessary than ever before to build a bridge across a divide that has been developing between science and faith—necessary for the hope and future of the biosphere and its life, including our own. It is necessary in our time because we now are reaping the Earth-degrading consequences of this continued division. Many religious people, especially those who take the Bible seriously, distance themselves from science, a phenomenon that began in 1859 with Darwin's *Origin of Species*. With this distancing, with this fragmentation of disciplines, has come a corresponding fragmentation of how we conceive the world.

What we need now to ensure a livable Earth is bridge-building and a "defragmention" of the disciplines and our dealings with the world—all in response to what the Earth and its climate system and hydrologic cycles are telling us. Unless we bridge the divide, we will not be able to address the great environmental degradations and transformations that threaten our planet and its life, including our own lives.

We human creatures are part of the great economy of creation, and we also are its stewards. We have divine appointments to safeguard the integrity of creation and sustain and renew the life of the Earth. Unfolding in the canon of scripture, vindicated in Christ's resurrection, and celebrated in the Eucharist, this economy is the comprehensive context of Christian mission today. May we be faithful in our work and life within this economy, from which our lives receive vital support and to whose services we return with service of our own.

Calvin B. DeWitt *is a professor of environmental studies at the University of Wisconsin in Madison and president emeritus of Au Sable Institute, which helps prepare undergraduate and graduate students for environmental careers. A scientist, writer, and conservationist, he is particularly interested in helping Christian colleges and universities across the continent and globe teach environmental stewardship. DeWitt's work is chiefly focused on building bridges between environmental science, ethics, and practice. He has given convocation lectures at more than seventy U.S. and Canadian colleges and universities and has brought his message worldwide through travels to China, Korea, India, Indonesia, Malaysia, Mexico, Russia, Ecuador, the Dominican Republic, and the United Kingdom. Among his many publications are* Earth-Wise: A Biblical Response to Environmental Issues *(2008) and* Caring for Creation: Responsible Stewardship of God's Handiwork *(1998).*

Song of Salmon

David James Duncan

In 2001, I published a book called *My Story as told by Water*, about my lifelong love for rivers and wild salmon. When the book won a following, even a few priests, preachers, and theologians began to sing its praises; the religion editor of one of the West's fatter newspapers noticed, and phoned the Portland essayist Brian Doyle. This editor told Brian that some pagan named Duncan was crisscrossing the land preaching that salmon are essential to the Pacific Northwest's chain of life, its economy, its spiritual integrity, its Christian theology, and its culture.

"I know the man," said Doyle.

"The guy claims," the editor grumbled, "that a diet of wild salmon flesh will cure mental illness, rejuvenate your sex life, inspire cold-turkey abstinence from network TV and partisan politics, and unite the human heart with the kingdoms of nature and of heaven. I'm concerned that this could damage the number of subscriptions to our fine fat violent newspaper."

"If more salmon come," said Brian, "we'll keep subscribing to have something to wrap our fresh salmon in."

"Duncan gets on a high horse," the editor groused. "For instance, he calls salmon 'divine gifts created in an unending Beginning' and 'a product less of evolution than of unconditional love.'"

"He's a Scot," replied Brian, "a people famed for strong stances. The Scots flavor their whiskies with dirt. They fish with seventeen-foot rods. Their men wear skirts. They eat haggis for godsake. But they do love their salmon. Maybe it's love that makes Duncan's horse so high and mighty."

Brian's grasp of us Scots is rooted in his Irishness. The Irish make their whiskies out of spud lymph. They kiss an unhygienic stone for luck. They play their pipes with their armpits. They're too busy scraping fiddles to fish with any length of rod. Their men don't wear kilts but their women wear the pants. They envy the Scots terribly. But they're our ancient cousins and love the salmon as we do. So when the editor hired Brian to interview me, I was pleased.

The question we were to debate was whether it is theologically accurate to say that wild salmon are *holy*. The trouble with this plan was, I've spent thousands of days on rivers awestruck by this very holiness. So for me debate is not possible. My certainty as to the holiness of salmon long ago achieved the kind of vehemence we associate with Old Testament prophets. Indeed, upon learning of our debate topic I simply asked Brian, who's Catholic, if he were well enough connected in Rome to get my views on salmon's holiness published in some obscure corner of the Bible.

Brian furrowed his brow. "Where might you sneak it in?" he asked.

"How about: Joshua, Judges, Ruth, Samuel, Kings, Coho?" I suggested.

"Those who notice will object," said he.

"Rome makes new saints," I argued. "They can sign off on a Song of Salmon!"

"Rome is not Scotland," Brian warned.

So we settled for the newspaper, that day. Brian began our interview by asking, "How is a wild chinook salmon the size of your leg a holy creature?" My answer wasn't mine at all: it was Christianity's and salmon's answer, and way bigger than any of us, so the pride I take in it isn't self-pride: it's salmon pride.

"Salmon are holy," I replied, "because on the Bible's very first page God says, *"Let the waters bring forth abundantly the moving creature that hath life. . . . And God created great whales and fishes and every living creature that moveth, which the waters brought forth abundantly, after their kind, and God saw that it was good, and blessed them, saying, Be fruitful, and multiply, and fill the waters in the seas."* Does that sound like a description of an industrial pond full of tilapia or a brown tide of net-penned salmon-sewage? Salmon are holy because *"the Earth is the Lord's"* (Psalms), and because *"everything shall live whither the river cometh and the fish shall be exceeding many and ye shall inherit them, one as well as another"* (Ezekiel). Does that sound like the Snake River dams that have killed 90 percent of our divine inheritance in forty years? Salmon are holy because we humans were placed here as *"renters"* (Leviticus) and *"caretakers"* (Genesis), whom Jesus advised to steward earth, river, and sea *"on earth as it is in heaven"* (Luke, Mark, Matthew), as the Father who created all forms of life would have it.

Salmon are holy because they're the life's blood and beloveds of fisherfolk, and the first disciples of Christ were fisherfolk, so it's the trade of Peter, James, and John we're fighting to defend here. Salmon are formidably holy, because the commercial fisherman Peter guards the Pearly Gates. Salmon are holy because, when their flesh feeds even the most intractable salmon-haters among us, they are literally "loving their enemies and doing good to those who hate them." Salmon are holy because, when they feed their young bodies to kingfishers and otters and eagles; and their larger ocean-going bodies to seals, sea lions, and orcas; and their magnificent, sex-driven, returned-to-the-river bodies to bears and Indian tribes and sport and commercial fishers and fly fishers; and finally even their spawned-out nitrogen-rich bodies to salmonberry bushes, sword ferns, cedar trees, and wildflowers, they have served us from one end of their lives to the other as a kind of living gospel in themselves.

Wild Pacific salmon of all six species have forever climbed our rivers like the heroes of some wondrous poem or song, nailing their shining bodies to lonely beds of gravel not for anything *they* stand to gain, but that tiny silver offspring and three hundred salmon-eating species of flora and fauna may live and thrive. When these blessings come no longer, the Northwest's living image of self-sacrifice goes silent: no more sermon. As the father of three children to whom I yearn to pass down the sense that their hearts are heroic and their souls immortal, I find the silence of salmonless rivers *very* hard to bear. So I've decided on this: I will stop fighting for wild salmon on the same day that wild salmon stop trying to migrate hundreds of miles and climb thousands of feet back into their birth streams.

Fishers all know it; we've all felt it in the power surging into our hands and bodies through our fishing rods: they'll never quit. Song of Salmon forever!

David James Duncan is a novelist and essayist whose work has appeared in Harper's, The Sun, Orion, Gray's Sporting Journal, *and many other publications.* My Story as told by Water, *his memoir and meditation on living rivers, was a National Book Award finalist. His novel* The River Why *ranks among the hundred best books of the American West as named by the* San Francisco Chronicle, *and another novel,* The Brothers K, *was a* New York Times *Notable Book. His most recent nonfiction*

book (2006) is God Laughs and Plays. *Duncan speaks about restoring salmon and the West's wild rivers to a broad range of audiences including fishers, conservation groups, and congregations of many denominations. This essay is adapted from a talk given in 2007 to seven hundred tribal, commercial, sport, and fly fishers on the banks of the Willamette River in Portland, Oregon.*

Consider This

T. L. Gray

Recently I had the privilege of attending a private viewing of the film *An Inconvenient Truth*, featuring Al Gore. This viewing, held at Providence Missionary Baptist Church in Atlanta, Georgia, was open to all religious leaders within the community. The "truth" presented in this film was probably not what Jesus had in mind when he said, "You will know the truth and the truth will make you free." Nevertheless, many uninformed minds, including my own, were freed on that evening, and it was that truth which served as the catalyst for this sermon.

The psalmist David states in Psalm 8:3–4, "When I look at your heavens, the works of your finger, the moon and stars that you have established; what are human beings that you are mindful of them, mortals that you care for them?" The King James Version of this text begins, "When I consider thy heavens . . ." Somehow the poetic language of the King James Version seems to capture for me the true awe that David must have felt as he considered the vastness of the universe.

I can imagine David attempting to calculate the distance between the Earth and the farthest star, only to his disappointment. No doubt he attempted to articulate his emotions, but only to his frustration. And so we find David here in the text content to contemplate the incomprehensibility of God and God's universe. And David, as he lay there in that field that night, looking up into the heavens, sang this psalm, "When I consider thy heavens, the work of thy fingers, the moon and the stars, which thou ordained" (King James Version). The hymn writer Carl Boberg added on to this verse when he wrote, "Then sings my soul, my Savior God to thee, how great thou art, how great thou art!"

And so the question I pose to you today, my brothers and sisters, is, have you ever really taken the time to reverence God's creation? If you're like me, you probably haven't given it any real thought. After all, we can see the moon, the stars, the sun, and the universe daily, and unless we are prompted to take a closer look, the spectacular often begins to appear common.

Knowing this, I would like to look at Psalm 8:3 while simultaneously providing my critique of *An Inconvenient Truth*, so that we can gain both a greater appreciation of and greater knowledge about God's creation. My subject today is, Consider This! And I would like for you first to consider with me the issue of global warming.

Global warming is the gradual increase of the Earth's temperature. Now if you've ever lived in Chicago, New York, Wisconsin, Ohio, Maine, New Jersey, or Philadelphia, you may think: praise the Lord! What could be wrong with an additional week of spring or one less week of winter? Furthermore, there has to be something morally and ethically wrong with ten-degree weather and a minus-thirty-degree windchill factor. God can't be pleased with that.

However, while individuals in Chicago and New York may be elated that they have yet to see a flake of snow this winter, and are rejoicing over some of the warmest days in January they have ever seen, the issue before us is still one worthy of great concern. Global warming is one of the most important issues in the world today. Equally as important as world peace, race reconciliation, poverty, oppression, bipartisanship, religious tolerance, and the war in Iraq, global warming, my brothers and sisters, threatens our very existence.

And today as I stand before you, I'm not as concerned that this topic is being overlooked by the government and by politicians as I am with the fact that the church is overlooking this issue also. Al Gore put it best when he said, "This is not a political issue, but rather this is a moral issue." And the last time I checked, the church was still in the business of morality. Not the business of gossiping, not the business of networking, and not the business of capitalism, but rather the church is supposed to be in the business of morality.

Global warming is a result of unrestrained burning of fossil fuels, the destruction of entire forests, the development of power plants, and ultimately the blatant disregard by humans for the Earth and the environment—and therefore I contend that this is an issue of morality. The ramifications have been devastating, and the consequences have been cataclysmic.

Consider, if you would, the following. The number of category-5 hurricanes, such as Katrina, Rita, and Wilma, has almost doubled in the last thirty years as a result of warming temperatures in oceans. Malaria has spread to higher altitudes in places like the Colombian Andes due to melting ice. Ten of the hottest years on record occurred within the last fourteen years, causing record numbers of heat-related deaths worldwide. The Arctic ice cap has diminished by 40 percent in the last forty years, causing flooding and destroying entire sea-level communities. And, for the first time in history, polar bears are actually drowning because they cannot find ice in the ocean where they can rest.

If this rapid warming continues, heat waves will be more frequent and more intense. Heat-related deaths will double in just twenty-five years, to more than three hundred thousand yearly. Droughts and wildfires will occur more often. More than a million species worldwide could be driven to extinction. Global sea levels could rise by more than twenty feet, devastating coastal areas worldwide. And the Arctic Ocean could be ice-free within fifty years.

These statistics should be frightening to anyone and everyone who hears them, and they demand a response from the church. It is incumbent upon us, as stewards over God's creation, to speak up for those who cannot speak up for themselves, as well as that which cannot speak up for itself. We must expose the truth: that global warming is a direct result of disrespect and disregard for and the degradation of God's creation. After all, it was God who created the heavens, and it was God who created the Earth. As stewards over God's creation, then, we must respect and reverence what God has entrusted unto us. And I would venture to say that the one of the pervasive problems in society today is the lack of awe and reverence for God and God's creation.

What David teaches us in Psalm 8:3 is the importance of meditating not only on the God of creation but also on the creation of God. For it is in creation that we see God and know God. Paul even tells us in Romans that, since the very creation of the world, God's eternal power has been understood through the things God has made. But what is it that would cause a person to love and worship God, yet destroy what God has made? Any father who, upon receiving a handmade birthday card from his five-year-old son, proceeded to ball it up in the child's face would be called cruel. Any woman who, upon receiving a dozen roses from her husband, threw them in the trash would be called uncaring. And likewise, I propose that any people who, upon receiving a beautiful Earth from the Creator, proceed to destroy it and render it unlivable can be called ungrateful.

Now, let me reassure you that my intention is not to proclaim damnation or destruction; I am not a doom-and-gloom preacher. Neither have I come to prophesy pandemonium or to incite feelings of fear and nihilism. Rather, I have come with good news. Good news that, although all these events are possible, they are not inevitable. For not only is hope still possible but also the calling is clear: we must begin to take care of the Earth. We must also begin to inform, instruct, and initiate a greater respect and a greater reverence for creation.

Well, the question you're no doubt asking is, how? And so, as I close my message, I ask once more if you would consider this. Consider what could be if everyone decided to write their elected officials and demand that legislation be passed to mandate cleaner cars and cleaner power plants. If everyone decided to purchase hybrid vehicles, or if everyone who could bought a car instead of a truck. If everyone carpooled back and forth to work and took public transportation on the weekend. If everyone would simply replace their incandescent lightbulbs with compact fluorescent bulbs. Consider the difference a little can make if we all decided to make a difference.

The average American generates about fifteen thousand pounds of carbon dioxide every year—from personal transportation and home energy use, and from the energy used to produce all the products each person consumes daily. And most of us are not considering any of this. The United States is the number one producer of carbon dioxide, and although we make up just 4 percent of the world's population, we produce 25 percent of the carbon dioxide pollution from fossil fuel burning—more than China, India, and Japan combined. And so, my brothers and sisters, my friends and colleagues, I submit to you today that this is a moral issue with ghastly implications. For these reasons, I admonish you to consider this before it's too late.

T. L. Gray is a doctoral student in ethics and society at Vanderbilt University. He received his bachelor of arts in religion from Trinity International University, his master of divinity degree from Morehouse School of Religion and the Interdenominational Theological Center and his master of sacred theology degree from Boston University School of Theology. He is also a licensed minister in the National Baptist Convention USA. His interests focus on the areas of pragmatism, political and environmental ethics, social justice, and homiletics.

Beyond Civilization

Abraham Joshua Heschel

Technical civilization is the product of labor, of man's exertion of power for the sake of gain, for the sake of producing goods. It begins when man, dissatisfied with what is available in nature, becomes engaged in a struggle with the forces of nature in order to enhance his safety and to increase his comfort. To use the language of the Bible, the task of civilization is to subdue the Earth, to have dominion over the beast.

How proud we often are of our victories in the war with nature, proud of the multitude of instruments we have succeeded in inventing, of the abundance of commodities we have been able to produce. Yet our victories have come to resemble defeats. In spite of our triumphs, we have fallen victims to the work of our hands; it is as if the forces we had conquered have conquered us.

Is our civilization a way to disaster, as many of us are prone to believe? Is civilization essentially evil, to be rejected and condemned? The faith of the Jew is not a way out of this world but a way of being within and above this world; not to reject but to surpass civilization. The Sabbath is the day on which we learn the art of *surpassing* civilization.

Adam was placed in the Garden of Eden "to dress it and to keep it" (Genesis 2:15). Labor is not only the destiny of man; it is endowed with divine dignity. However, after he ate of the tree of knowledge, he was condemned to toil, not only to labor: "In toil shall thou eat . . . all the days of thy life" (Genesis 3:17). Labor is a blessing, toil is the misery of man.

The Sabbath as a day of abstaining from work is not a depreciation but an affirmation of labor, a divine exaltation of its dignity. *Thou shalt abstain from labor on the seventh day* is a sequel to the command: *Six days shalt thou labor, and do all thy work.*

"Six days shalt thou labor and do all thy work; but the seventh day is Sabbath unto the Lord thy God. Just as we are commanded to keep the Sabbath, we are commanded to labor. "Love work . . ." The duty to work for six days is just as much a part of God's covenant with man as the duty to abstain from work on the seventh day.

To set apart one day a week for freedom, a day on which we would not use the instruments which have been so easily turned into weapons of destruction, a day for being with ourselves, a day of detachment from the vulgar, of independence of external obligations, a day on which we stop worshipping the idols of technical civilization, a day on which we use no money, a day of armistice in the economic struggle with our fellow men and the forces of nature—is there any institution that holds out a greater hope for man's progress than the Sabbath?

The solution of mankind's most vexing problem will not be found in renouncing technical civilization, but in attaining some degree of independence of it.

In regard to external gifts, to outward possessions, there is only one proper attitude—to have them and to be able to do without them. On the Sabbath we live, as it were, *independent of technical civilization*: we abstain primarily from any activity that aims at remaking or reshaping the things of space. Man's royal privilege to conquer nature is suspended on the seventh day.

What are the kinds of labor not to be done on the Sabbath? They are, according to the ancient rabbis, all those acts which were necessary for the construction and furnishing of the Sanctuary in the desert. The Sabbath itself is a sanctuary which we build, *a sanctuary in time.*

It is one thing to race or be driven by the vicissitudes that menace life, and another thing to stand still and to embrace the presence of an eternal moment.

The seventh day is the armistice in man's cruel struggle for existence, a truce in all conflicts, personal and social, peace between man and man, man and nature, peace within man; a day on which handling money is considered a desecration, on which man avows his independence of that which is the world's chief idol. The seventh day is the exodus from tension, the liberation of man from his own muddiness, the installation of man as a sovereign in the world of time.

In the tempestuous ocean of time and toil, there are islands of stillness where man may enter a harbor and reclaim his dignity. The island is the seventh day, the Sabbath, a day of detachment from things, instruments, and practical affairs as well as of attachment to the spirit.

The Sabbath must all be spent "in charm, grace, peace, and great love[,] . . . for on it even the wicked in hell find peace." It is, therefore, a double sin to show anger on the Sabbath. "Ye shall kindle no fire throughout your habitations on the Sabbath day" (Exodus 35:3) is interpreted to mean: "Ye shall kindle no fire of controversy nor the heat of anger." Ye shall kindle no fire—not even the fire of righteous indignation.

Out of the days through which we fight and from whose ugliness we ache, we look to the Sabbath as our homeland, as our source and destination. It is a day in which we abandon our plebeian pursuits and reclaim our authentic state, in which we may partake of a blessedness in which we are what we are, regardless of whether we are learned or not, of whether our career is a success or a failure; it is a day of independence of social conditions.

All week we may ponder and worry whether we are rich or poor, whether we succeed or fail in our occupations, whether we accomplish or fall short of reaching our goals. But who could feel distressed when gazing at spectral glimpses of eternity, except to feel startled at the vanity of being so distressed?

The Sabbath is no time for personal anxiety or care, for any activity that might dampen the spirit of joy. The Sabbath is no time to remember sins, to confess, to repent, or even to pray for relief or anything we might need. It is a day for praise, not a day for petitions. Fasting, mourning, demonstrations of grief are forbidden. The period of mourning is interrupted by the Sabbath. And if one visits the sick on the Sabbath, one should say: "It is the Sabbath, one must not complain; you will soon be cured." One must abstain from toil and strain on the seventh day, even from strain in the service of God.

Why are the Eighteen Benedictions not recited on the Sabbath? It is because the Sabbath was given to us by God for joy, for delight, for rest, and should not be marred by worry or grief. Should there be a sick one in the household, we might remember this while reciting the benediction "Heal the sick," and would become saddened and gloomy on the Sabbath day. It is for this same reason that we recite in the Sabbath grace after meals the request that "there be no sadness or trouble in the day of our rest." It is a sin to be sad on the Sabbath day.

For the Sabbath is a day of harmony and peace, peace between man and man, peace within man, and peace with all things. On the seventh day man has no right to tamper with God's world, to change the state of physical things. It is a day of rest for *man and animal* alike:

In it thou shalt not do any manner of work, thou, nor thy son, nor thy daughter, nor thy man-servant, nor thy maidservant, nor thine ox, nor thine ass, nor any of thy *cattle*, nor thy stranger that is within thy gates; that thy man-servant and thy maid-servant may rest as well as thou.

Rabbi Solomon of Radomsk once arrived in a certain town, where, he was told, lived an old woman who had known the famous Rabbi Elimelech. She was too old to go out, so he went to see her and asked her to tell him what she knew about the great Master.

I do not know what went on in his room, because I worked as one of the maids in the kitchen of his house. Only one thing I can tell you. During the week the maids would often quarrel with one another, as is common. But, week after week, on Friday when the Sabbath was about to arrive, the spirit in the kitchen was like the spirit on the eve of the Day of Atonement. Everybody would be overcome with an urge to ask forgiveness of each other. We were all seized by a feeling of affection and inner peace.

The Sabbath, thus, is more than an armistice, more than an interlude; it is a profound conscious harmony of man and the world, a sympathy for all things, and a participation in the spirit that unites what is below and what is above. All that is divine in the world is brought into union with God. This is Sabbath, and the true happiness of the universe.

"Six days shall thou labor and do all thy work" (Exodus

20:8). Is it possible for a human being to do all his work in six days? Does not our work always remain incomplete? What the verse means to convey is: Rest on the Sabbath as if all your work were done. Another interpretation: *Rest even from the thought of labor.*

A pious man once took a stroll in his vineyard on the Sabbath. He saw a breach in the fence, and then determined to mend it when the Sabbath would be over. At the expiration of the Sabbath he decided: "Since the thought of repairing the fence occurred to me on the Sabbath, I shall never repair it."

Abraham Joshua Heschel (1907–1972) was a Polish-born, German-educated theologian and philosopher. Deported by the Nazis in 1938, by 1945 he had made his way to the Jewish Theological Seminary in New York, where he taught until his death. He wrote, taught, and worked to revive and renew mystical, prophetic, and active dimensions of Jewish piety and practice. He stressed experience, feeling, and lively personal response in spirituality, and was a leader in American civil rights and anti–Vietnam War activism.

The Great Without

Linda Hogan

In European natural histories, human imagination was most often projected onto the outside world. Pliny the Elder's *Natural History*, for instance, was an errant map of this true world. There were dog-headed humans who could only bark, men with heads in their chests, and people with only one foot who nonetheless were able to leap powerfully and to use the foot as a shade tree. There were mermaids, springs believed to grant eternal life, and islands where demons or angels lived. At one time the Egyptians thought that people on the other side of the world walked upside down. Bestiaries included the phoenix, griffins, and unicorns. Largely unshaped by fact, knowledge, or even observation, these fantasy worlds became the world as seen by the human mind.

The relationship between nature and humanity posed a dilemma. At one time it was thought that the world entered the human eye, and that only through our seeing of it did it exist. There was much discussion about how a mountain could fit into the human eye. This difficulty with perspective pushed humans toward other conclusions just as erroneous as believing foremost in the eye of the beholder. Euclid thought that the eye was the point of origin for all things. Plato believed that the world emanated from the eye, while others thought that objects gave off something by which we perceived them. In any case, most theories made nature smaller than it is and made the human larger. Vision was about the seer only, not the seen.

Nothing could be more different from how tribal people on all continents have seen the world. From the perspectives of those who have remained in their own terrain for thousands of years, there were—and are—other points of view. For tribal thinkers, the outside world creates the human: we are alive to the interactions of nature outside the self. It is a more humble, and far more steady, way to view the world. Nature is the creator, not the created.

There exists, too, a geography of spirit that is tied to and comes from the larger geography of nature. It offers to humans the bounty and richness of the world. Father Berard Haile, a priest traveling among the Navajo in the 1930s, was in awe of the complexity of their knowledge of their ecosystem. In his book about the healing ceremony the Upward Moving Way, he describes the Navajo knowledge of plants: the movement of stalks upward as the roots deepen, the insects beneath and above the ground, the species of birds that come to this plant. All aspects of the ceremony reveal a wide knowledge of the world. In order for healing to take place, this outside life and world must be taken in and "seen" by the patient as being part of one working system.

Laurens van der Post, a writer, naturalist, and psychologist who grew up in Africa, wrote in his essay "The Great Uprooter" about how his son's illness was announced by a dream. In the dream, the young man stood on a beach, unable to move, watching a great tidal wave of water bearing down on him. From out of the wave, a large black elephant walked toward him. This dream, van der Post was certain, announced his son's cancer, the first point of cellular change. Van der Post called the dream something that came from "the great without": such an experience seemed to encompass, he said, all the withouts and withins a human could experience.

Nature is now too often defined by people who are fragmented from the land. This broken world is seldom one that carries the human spirit. Too rarely is it understood that the soul lies at all points of intersection between human consciousness and all the rest of nature. Skin is hardly a container. Our boundaries are not solid; we are permeable, and even when we are solitary dreamers we are rooted in the soul outside. If we are open enough, strong enough to connect with the world, we become something greater than we are.

The Lakota writer Zitkala-Sa (Gertrude Simmons Bonnin) wrote of the separation between humankind and the natural world as a great loss to her. In her book *American Indian Stories*, published in 1921, she said that nature could have helped her to survive her forced removal to an Indian boarding school.

> I was ready to curse men of small capacity for being the dwarfs their God had made them. In the process of my education I had lost all consciousness of the nature world about me. Thus, when a hidden rage took me to the small white-walled prison which I then called my room, I unknowingly turned away from my own salvation. For the white man's papers, I had given up my faith in the Great Spirit. For these same papers I had forgotten the healing in trees and brooks. Like a slender tree, I had been uprooted from my mother, nature, and God.

Zitkala-Sa might have agreed with Pliny that there were dog-headed, barking men, and men with heads, not hearts, in their chests.

Soul loss—called *susto* in contemporary North American Hispanic communities—is what happens as the world around us disappears. It is a common condition in the modern world. *Susto* probably began when the soul was banished from nature, when humanity withdrew from the world, when there was a division into two realms—human and nature, animate and inanimate, sentient and not. This was when the soul first began to slip away and crumble.

Anthropologist Michael Harner wrote about healing methods among indigenous people relocated to an urban slum.

In the reversal and healing of soul loss, Brazilian tribal people who have tragically lost their land and their place in the world visit or reimagine nature in order to become well again. The healing takes place in the forest at night, as the person is returned for a while to the land he or she once knew. Such people are often cured through their renewed connections, their "visions of the river forest world, including visions of animals, snakes, and plants." Unfortunately, these places are now only ghosts of what they once were.

The cure for *susto*, soul sickness, is not in books. It is written in the bark of a tree, in the moonlit silence of night, in the bank of a river and the water's motion. The cure is outside ourselves.

In the 1500s, Paracelsus, considered by many to be a father of modern medicine, was greatly disliked by his contemporaries. For a while, though, he almost returned the practice of medicine to its wider context of relationships by emphasizing the importance of harmony between man and nature. His view of healing is in keeping with the one tribal elders still hold, that a human being is a small model of the world and the universe. Vast spaces stretch inside us, he thought, an inner firmament as large as the outer world.

The world inside the mind is lovely sometimes, and large. Its existence is why a person can recall the mist of morning clouds on a hill, the fern forest, and the black skies of night that the Luiseño (a tribe who lived at the time of first contact in what is now coastal southern California) called their spirit, acknowledging that the soul of the world is great within the human soul. This is an enlarged and generous sense of self, life, and being—as if not only is the body a creation of the world elements, but also air and light and night sky have created an inner vision that some have called a map of the cosmos. In Lakota astronomy, the stars are called the breath of the Great Spirit. It is as if the old Lakota foresaw physics and modern astronomy—sciences that now tell us we are the transformed matter of stars, that the human body is a kind of cosmology.

The inward may have been, all along, the wrong direction to seek. A person seems so small, and without is the river, the mountain, the forest of fern and tree, the desert with its lizards, the glacial meltings and freezings, and the movements of life. The cure for soul loss is in the mist of morning, the grass that grew a little through the night, the first warmth of sunlight, the walking human in a world infused with intelligence and spirit.

Linda Hogan *(Chickasaw) is an internationally recognized public speaker and author of poetry, fiction, and essays. Her recent books include* Rounding the Human Corners *and* People of the Whale *(both 2008). She also authored the novels* Mean Spirit, *which won the Oklahoma Book Award and the Mountains and Plains Book Award, and was a Pulitzer Prize finalist;* Solar Storms, *a finalist for the International Impact Award; and*

Power. *Her volume of poetry,* The Book of Medicines, *was a finalist for the National Book Critics Circle Award, and her poetry also has been honored with the Colorado Book Award, a Minnesota State Arts Grant, an American Book Award, and a Lannan Fellowship. Hogan's nonfiction includes* Dwellings, a Spiritual History of the Land; The Woman Who Watches Over the World: A Native Memoir; *and, with Brenda Peterson,* Sightings, The Mysterious Journey of the Gray Whale. *She has edited several anthologies on nature and spirituality and wrote the script for* Everything Has a Spirit, *a PBS documentary on American Indian religious freedom. In addition, Hogan has received a National Endowment for the Arts Fellowship, a Guggenheim, and the Mountains and Plains Lifetime Achievement Award. She has been inducted into the Chickasaw Hall of Fame.*

A professor emerita at the University of Colorado, Hogan currently lives in Oklahoma and holds the post of writer in residence for the Chickasaw Nation. Environmental issues are the major focus in all of her work, writing, and teaching.

One Pastor's Question and Hope

Joel C. Hunter

"Why is it that sometimes nonbelievers are more ready to do the right thing than believers?" That's what I asked my congregation when I preached about Jonah, noting that Nineveh is more willing to repent than Jonah is.

Because I am involved with environmental groups, I can look around to see a good number of caring and principled people seeking to preserve the gift of creation. But the evangelicals, my particular part of the family of God, are lagging behind. We believe in the authority of scripture in our lives. We know that the first order from God we as a human race received was given to Adam in Genesis 2:15: to care for the Earth. "Cultivate [develop] and keep [protect] it," he said. Yet somehow we have linked this clear command with a risky political stand or an undesirable social affiliation. Amazing.

So I decided to communicate some important principles to my congregation. I knew I would need to answer three questions: What is the theological basis for prioritizing the care of creation? What are the facts that make this action urgent? What can we do about it?

But first, I would need to remember the reason I was personally passionate about God's creation.

One day long ago I was playing in my backyard. I'm not sure why I was alone that early afternoon; maybe all the other kids had to take naps or were eating a dessert they didn't want to share.

It was a sunny, hot, and particularly still day. I remember this because it was so uncomfortable that I was wishing for some sort of breeze to cool me off. So I lay down in the grass and looked up at a cloudless sky, then at our silver maple tree—so called because the tops of the leaves were green, but the bottoms were more of a silver-gray-green color.

I don't know how thoughts come to the mind of a bored eight-year-old. I just remember thinking, "I wonder if there really is a God?" Then I remember praying, "God, if you really exist, would you somehow let me know?" At that very moment a wind—not a breeze but an almost violent wind—turned every leaf on that maple tree from drooping green to flashing silver, and the wind kept blowing for at least ten seconds. It was beautiful, startling, and momentary. The wind did not blow again. Once was enough for me.

I wonder, even now, how many times God still makes himself known to people through creation. He did it many times in the Bible: through a parting sea, a (non)burning bush, a ram caught in the thicket when a son could have been killed, and often through the awesome grandeur of creation's natural beauty.

I have come to realize that the protection of creation is not just for practical purposes, but also for inspirational ones. Creation is how I first believed; I want to keep those earthy sermons going. Toward that end, I want my congregation to develop a sense of transcendence, not just an obedience to scriptural mandates or an obligation to love our neighbors enough to care about their environment.

The worship of God requires a taste for that which is beyond the material, practical, and even religious practices required for us to thrive. Worship is about a soul's connection that goes beyond the mind or body. The development of that connection, I have found, depends much upon one's sense of beauty.

We get the picture of God as artist when we see him evaluate his work in Genesis 2:31: "God saw all that He had made, and behold, it was very good." The Hebrew word translated here as "very good" is not just a term of moral evaluation but also implies "fitting." In other words, it is an appraisal of symmetry and beauty as well as functionality.

Remember how Jesus appreciated the beauty of nature and told his disciples to do the same: "And why are you worried about clothing? Observe how the lilies of the field grow; they do not toil or spin, yet I say to you that not even Solomon in all his glory clothed himself as one of these" (Matthew 5: 28–29). This passage is not merely about anxiety control: it speaks of the kind of relaxation and trust that can come only with an appreciation for the beauty and wonder of nature. This is not a mental adjustment; it is a spiritual exercise to connect us to the Creator.

Creation care is a spiritual practice that develops the soul when we take time to appreciate the awesome capabilities and imagination of the Creator.

In addition to the very clear initial command from God to be good managers of his creation (as if we needed any moral mandate beyond that), there are numerous biblical or theological reasons to be avid environmentalists. I will name only a few:

God looks upon all He has made and deems it "very good" (Genesis 1:31). If it has moral and esthetic goodness, are we then excused in treating the Earth as merely a utilitarian resource to be exploited?

God makes a covenant to preserve not only human beings but also "every living creature" (Genesis 9:11–12). If God cares about the generations of all species, what implication does this have for the pollution that destroys them?

Jesus taught us that, second only to loving God with our whole heart, loving our neighbor as ourselves (Matthew 22:29) *is paramount.* Our neighbors, especially the poor, are endangered by environmental degradation, much of it caused by our cavalier overconsumption. What will we say to him, come the time of judgment (Matthew 25:40)?

I want my congregation to know that protecting and appreciating the environment are important for these reasons—and that harming the Earth is more than simply a problem to be fixed for our own well-being.

What would keep any Christian from wanting to conserve and admire nature, which seems like simple common sense? One aspect of the environmental crisis has generated so much controversy and polarization that many Christians would rather debate it than participate in creation care: global warming.

The world's most authoritative body on this subject, the Intergovernmental Panel on Climate Change (an international consortium of scientists and policy experts), has made it abundantly clear that anthropogenic causes are speeding global warming, and speeding us toward an unprecedented catastrophe. There are some credible contrarian voices, which is as it should be. Debate keeps us honest. Yet there are also politicians, pundits, and preachers who benefit (in so many ways) from polarization. Therefore, some would rather keep talking than take action. I want my congregation to know the facts that science has demonstrated, and that show the extent to which climate change threatens the future of everything and everyone on Earth.

Almost every Christian I have talked to, no matter where he or she stands on the global warming issue, starts out the conversation with: "Of course we should be good stewards of creation. . . ." Great. Let's then accomplish that stated ideal with practical steps any person or group can take:

On the personal level, creation care is a challenge to which each person can make an immediate and ongoing response. I issued to my congregation a personal action list focusing on the three Rs: *recycle* or repair (car maintenance, for example); *replace* (lightbulbs, appliances, and the like) with energy-efficient products; and *reduce* energy usage (turn thermostats down, drive the speed limit or under, and so on).

On the church level, every church or organization can lower its environmental pollution through a group effort. My local church did an audit (which ran to 122 pages of observations, suggestions, and benchmarks) to set progressive goals for reducing our carbon footprint.

On the policy-influencing level, my church members are becoming aware of how our voices can move local and state and national policy toward better stewardship of the environment. We are paying attention to every candidate's stand on the environment.

As a pastor, I came to the realization that the congregation will follow my lead. I have an obligation to be informed and vocal, or the people I lead are not likely to follow God in this area of moral obedience and neighbor-loving service.

I am fairly new to environmentalism as a moral issue. I got involved because some friends of mine, for whom I have great respect, were looking for national evangelical leaders to sign a document called the Evangelical Climate Initiative. My first response was, "I don't know anything about this subject; let me do some research." I love to study, and not long into the research I was saying to myself, "How in the world have I missed this?" Seeing that this issue has such potential for societal harm but also for spiritual good, I began to ask, "What else am I missing?"

I tell you this story to remind myself that the newly converted are usually the most obnoxious, and to assure you that there is no room for stone-throwing in my attitude. But those of us who are pastors and spiritual leaders do have influence on those we lead, and we are also the most likely to have an effect on other leaders.

Here are some ways to get informed and to carry through by adopting better practices as you lead your congregations. In addition, you can help other leaders in this area in the following ways:

Get involved with a faith-based group that works on environmental matters, so that your congregation learns to use creation care as a form of spiritual growth, rather than as a political choice or even merely as the right thing to do. If you are an evangelical Christian, the Evangelical Environmental Network is a good starting place. If you are from another faith or another branch of Christianity, you can probably find a faith-based affinity group.

Teach on the subject. You will grow more in your personal practice and intellectual knowledge if you have to teach others how to be a steward of God's creation—and why it is important.

Recruit volunteers from your congregation to form a task force. If they meet on a continuing basis, they will lead the church's efforts to improve creation care and take the main responsibility for it off the pastor's shoulders.

Most of all, make this effort part of a balanced approach to expressing the caring of Christ. Any of us can become caught up in a particular issue and thus, paradoxically, provoke more resistance than cooperation. A fanatic has been described as "one who won't change his mind and won't let you change the subject." Following Christ's teachings broadly, in ways that will benefit all the families of the Earth, will add to our credibility and effectiveness in caring for creation.

Let's help build a great spiritual and natural environment.

Dr. Joel C. Hunter is senior pastor of Northland, A Church Distributed, a congregation of twelve thousand that meets at several physical sites throughout central Florida and at more than one thousand virtual worship sites worldwide via the Internet. A longtime bridge builder who seeks common ground for the common good, Dr. Hunter has become an internationally known spokesperson for "compassion issues" outlined in scripture.

A respected leader in the evangelical community, Dr. Hunter is also working with respected members of the scientific community, as well as national organizations, including the Evangelical Climate Initiative and the Evangelical Environmental Network, to call attention to threats to the environment. In 2006, he made national headlines by joining dozens of evangelical Christian leaders in issuing a historic call to action on global warming. He was recently named organizing director of First Green Bank, which promotes environmental responsibility by offering lower interest rates for commercial projects that earn green building certification. Grist magazine has listed him among the top fifteen religious environmental leaders in the world, along with Pope Benedict XVI and the Dalai Lama.

Reborn in the Flames

Nandini Iyer

There is hardly any religion in which fire does not play a significant role. Fire and its alter egos—light, heat, the sun—are almost universal signifiers of divinity, sanctity, wisdom, creativity, and purification. At the same time, human beings have always been awed, even terrified, by the lethal, cruelly omnivorous power of fire. It blesses and brings life but also destroys, transforms, and kills.

In many creation myths, fire is the firstborn of heaven, the primordial link between God and the universe. In Genesis, light is the first creation, the eldest child of God's Word. In one of the most famous Vedic creation accounts, the Hymn of Creation, what first arises from the Great Divine Absolute, the Ground of Being, is warmth (heat, creative fire); in other accounts the primordial emanation is divine radiance. But God in the Old Testament also destroys by fire, and in many religious myths the world ends in a mighty conflagration. In Hinduism, the paradoxical regenerative-destructive nature of fire pervades the myths, symbols, and iconography of the god Shiva. He destroys the worn out, the useless, the corrupt, and the obstructive in order to purify and regenerate. Life comes from death.

This intellectually stimulating paradox is harder to accept, however, when it touches our own lives. That we must learn the possibility of rebirth from the death of the old and the familiar is a great but difficult lesson. These truths were brought home to me, suddenly and with cruel force, when our house in Santa Barbara was destroyed, along with 566 others, by the Painted Cave Fire in 1990. That fire took one human life and destroyed animals and plants, homes, property, material possessions, and loved mementos with indifferent rage. For many of us, it also swept away our pride of accomplishment, our hard-won but superficial confidence in our invulnerability, and our fragile sense of identity.

At first, I was stunned, unable to realize the full import of the event. The fire's deadly fingers seemed to reach everywhere, tearing at the very fabric and fiber of our lives—ripping apart the seams and sending pieces flying in all directions. It seemed as if every drop of feeling had been wrung out of my life, leaving me dry and shriveled, empty, unable to comprehend what had happened.

When I first drove up into the hills to survey the devastation, the familiar, comfortable landscape had vanished. Even the colors had changed; no longer did I see the gray-green wild sage, shrubs, and chaparral. Gone were the live oaks, the occasional evergreens, the scattered eucalyptus and sycamores, leaving only a sad, desolate moonscape covered with a layer of light gray ashes. Charred, twisted trunks, the crooked bare branches of trees, and a few scrub bushes traced strange patterns in darker gray and black against the sky. And the light fragrance of wild fennel and sage was replaced by the acrid smell of smoke, spread in ghostly wisps from scattered, still-smoldering embers by little gusts of wind stirring the burnt ground—the smell of death, it seemed to me. The earth exuded grief, desolation, and hopelessness, reflecting and intensifying the same feelings that were overwhelming me. The scorched earth seemed to echo my sense of abandonment and loss of the foundations and supporting pillars of my everyday life.

Where my home had been, nothing remained but fragments—the rubble, it seemed at first, of a ruined existence. Two small things alone remained intact—a china teacup and a tiny pottery owl bought at a Native American reservation. Later, it occurred to me that these little objects had survived because both had already been through a firing process in an extremely hot oven. On the other hand, a thirty-inch bronze antique statue of the dancing Shiva Nataraja, which I was certain must have survived the fire, had not. It was melted almost completely, only a twisted lump of metal remaining, barely identifiable as the figure's torso. But the most heart-wrenching sight that met my eyes was a little wild rabbit lying dead in the driveway, legs stretched out as if running. Quite clearly it had been racing for its life when caught in midflight and instantly incinerated by the fire.

Only after a while, when the initial shock and sorrow began to subside, did I start to reflect deeply on the fire's significance in the light of Hinduism—especially the symbolism of fire and the god Shiva, which I had lectured about so often in my classes on comparative religion.

I thought back to the many times when I had spoken with great fervor about detachment from the things of this world, especially material possessions, which every major religion emphasizes. How often I had talked, especially in relation to Hinduism and Buddhism, about the need to meet all events, whether pleasant or unpleasant, with equanimity and dispassion. How often I had cautioned my students about falling into the trap of identifying with the egotistic self, which gets overwhelmed, angry, and distraught, and even shatters, when things do not happen according to its own self-centered view of the world.

My mind slowly traveled to some of the fundamental beliefs and attitudes that underlie the Hindu worldview. In particular, I kept returning to the idea that the universe, being the manifestation of the energies of the Divine Absolute Godhead, is so suffused with divine life that all its apparently separate parts and beings are, in reality, inseparable. This idea naturally leads to a profoundly holistic, ecological viewpoint, in which all aspects of nature interconnect in such a way that harming one part creates a serious imbalance and disharmony that will eventually harm every other part. According to one creation myth, the Absolute Reality that is God breathes out the universe, which is made up of the innumerable breaths of the One. (These various ways of describing the universal supreme spirit are synonymous.) Each being is as unique as each breath, yet all are expressions of the same life breath. Yet another metaphor presents the universe as a vast and complex net whose crisscrossing strings form uncountable points of intersection, each knot adorned with a gem. In this view, each being is a precious gem and also a meeting point of connecting lines, which all interlink in an unbelievably complex pattern so that, directly or indirectly, each gem has a connection with every other, however remote. This is the marvelous, multilayered universe in which we find ourselves indissolubly and irrevocably linked with every other part of the whole. How, then, can we separate ourselves from other forms of life? Trying to disconnect, we end up straining and harming ourselves.

I began to see that the fire was not just about me and my feelings. Not only had hundreds of other human beings been affected, but so had vast numbers of animals and plants. A small part of the Earth itself had been scarred. But I had the opportunity, even the responsibility, to break out of my self-centered cage. I could refuse to isolate myself and instead consider the more universal meaning and implications of this disastrous fire.

A central belief in Hinduism is the law of karma. Neither fatalism nor determinism, which can lead to a defeatist inertia, karma is instead a law of ethical causation, implying that what human beings think and do sows the seeds of causes that will inevitably return to them as appropriate effects. The theory of karma emphasizes the importance of using one's free will to make rational and morally wise choices. To the extent that we have the capacity to reason, weigh alternatives, and make consciously right choices, we have a moral responsibility that other kingdoms of nature do not have. We should be acutely aware that the ripples of our actions (including the emotions, thoughts, and motives in which they are rooted) spread out in ever-widening circles that involve the lives of a myriad other creatures.

Hindu cosmology regards the universe as consisting of many levels of energy, from the subtlest to the grossest physical. The law of karma manifests on the physical plane as the laws of causation in natural science. But it also has parallels on the psychological, mental, and moral planes, and on all levels it works to restore the original harmony of the universe. As the Hindus believe the heart of the universe, the divine ground, to be love, peace, and harmony, karma is the law of ethical justice. It is impersonal, not dependent on the will of a personal deity, and it cannot be broken without dire consequences, any more than the physical laws of nature can be.

We can choose freely to acknowledge our oneness with nature or willfully set ourselves apart and act selfishly to fulfill our personal desires. The law of karma will take into account our external actions as well as the selfless (or selfish) motives behind them. In Hinduism, it seems clear that all of nature is sacred. To ignore this and disregard our oneness with nature, defining ourselves as the only important parts of the Earth, is to break the universal law of harmony and invite the inevitable and disastrous karmic consequences of this ignorant arrogance.

Also central to Hinduism is the embodiment of the sacred in the form of many deities. The highest Absolute Divine Reality, the God beyond God, is intuitively known in the profoundest depths of the immortal soul but unknowable and indescribable by the finite human mind. It can be dimly glimpsed by us only through personifications of its infinite qualities as manifested in the universe. The great elements of the natural world—earth, air, fire, and water—are symbolically personified as deities, as are the numberless phenomena in nature— the sun, moon, and planets; the rain, sky, rivers, dawn, and twilight; and many other earthly things that shape the cycles and rhythms of our lives. The abstract qualities and arts that give richness to human life are also seen as deities: love, justice, friendship, harmony, energy, creativity, knowledge, wisdom, prosperity, music, dance, and even death and infinity. These hundreds of Hindu gods and goddesses are not regarded as independent deities, but only as manifestations of the ultimate

Godhead, deriving their existence and power from the Divine Ground of Being.

Because the shock and sense of devastation that assaulted me came from fire, I was inevitably drawn to reflect on the many-layered symbolism associated with the god Shiva: the destroyer but also the regenerator, and (together with Brahma the creator and Vishnu the sustainer and preserver) part of the highest *trimurti*, or Divine Trinity. In particular, the powerful representations of Shiva as Nataraja, Lord of the Cosmic Dance, began to strike me with a new and deeper significance. For Shiva contains many contraries—destruction and regeneration, death and immortal life, and the darkness and inertia of primordial chaos as well as the dynamic light of creation. Out of darkness and death come light and new life. In this representation, Shiva's right foot is pressed down to destroy the ugly demon of heedlessness, ignorance, and selfishness.

Even more relevant to my distraught mind was the idea that Shiva's main symbol is fire, which nourishes, warms, and gives life but also destroys and devours. The figure of Shiva Nataraja is surrounded by a circle of flames—creative, divine, cosmic fire. In one of his right hands he holds a small flame, the sacred flame of the spirit, of devotion and self-sacrifice. For it is by the sacrifices we make for others—represented ritually by the incense, wood, flowers, and butter thrown into the Hindu ceremonial fire—that we are inwardly purified and regenerated. Fire, the transformer and purifier, is the essential core of every Hindu sacred ritual. Fire represents the divine, and the precious wood, incense, flowers, and butter thrown into the ceremonial fire represent the worshippers' faults and flaws—pride, anger, hatred, and greed, as well as cherished attachments and personal desires. All must be given up, "sacrificed," however painful it may be, if the individual is to be inwardly purified and uplifted. Through sacrifice in our lives, we are consumed by the fire of personal suffering, transformed and reborn at a higher level of being. We re-create ourselves by destroying negative emotions and desires that are as death to our inner selves.

As I meditated on these ideas, it dawned on me that the only way out of my shadow-filled desolation was to start detaching myself from the memory of my possessions, to see that I had an identity and life independent of them, and to try to emerge with fresh hope and a new sense of purpose.

The figure of Shiva illustrates a recurrent theme in Hinduism: that something has to die or be given up to create a new and perhaps richer life, a fresh birth. In nature this process is built in: the seed must be destroyed for the plant to be born. Many natural forest fires (which the Painted Cave Fire was not) occur when the old trees—crowding out young growth and cutting off nourishment, light, and life from saplings—are burned down, and the forest begins a new cycle of life. So, also, the person on a spiritual path must destroy through purification the selfish, separatist, egotistic self, with its unending desires and destructive emotions that alienate it from the rest of the world, so that the spiritual self can be born in the heart.

Our ruthless selfishness, given free rein, cuts us off not only from others but also from the divine, the source of light and life, and from the generous physical and psychological nourishment of nature in all its forms, which are suffused with spirit. Most of us are aware that the present global ecological crisis was brought on by our thoughtlessness and callow treatment of earth, air, fire (think of energy or fossil fuels), and water. We have engaged in greedy consumption of resources with no thought of renewing or restoring them. We have depleted and polluted the elements. Many practical and societal changes— economic, scientific, and environmental—are needed to address this. Hindu sages, however, would point out that we also need to look deeper into our hearts and minds and acknowledge that the problems of global warming and resource depletion are only outward symptoms of a deadly disease that our consciousness suffers from. Our self-preoccupation has cut us off from the only infinite, truly ever-renewable, self-generating source of life, energy, and nourishment—the Universal Spirit.

Hindu scriptures are replete with hymns of praise, invocations, and prayers of gratitude to the various deities that symbolize the myriad powers of God, who bestows endless, loving gifts upon us. The whole universe, we are told, arises from the sacrifice made by the gods, and we are asked to emulate them. We need to reconnect and restore our essential unity with nature—with the rest of humankind, animals and plants, and, yes, even the rocks and the Earth itself. But we cannot do this without rethinking realistically who and what we truly are, what is of real worth to our inner progress, our value system, and our priorities. Much of what we regard as necessary has no relevance to our true self, our spiritual growth, happiness, or well-being. Insofar as we are overcome with a thousand selfish desires, we are not free; we are held in bondage by our passions. Paradoxically, it is in our willingness to give up for others' sake—to sacrifice our separative tendencies in the fire that seems like the death of "me"—that we can be transformed and reborn. Loving others and nature with a sense of oneness gives us new life, a self that can know real contentment and harmony. As an ancient Hindu text says, "He who loves, lives; he who loves himself, lives in hell; he who loves another, lives on Earth; he who loves others, lives in heaven. But he who silently adores the Self of all creatures, lives in that Self, and It is eternal peace."

Nandini Iyer is an emeritus member of the Department of Religious Studies at the University of California, Santa Barbara. She was educated at the University of Bombay and the University of Oxford, taught philosophy at Oxford for eight years, and later cofounded the Institute of World Culture in California. She is coeditor of The Descent of the Gods: The Mystical Writings of A. E. *and has received special recognition from the U.S. Congress for "outstanding and invaluable service to the community" for her participation in and encouragement of interfaith and intercultural dialogue.*

What in Your Life Is Not for Sale?

Allen Johnson

"What took you so long?"

Larry Gibson's glaring eyes and set jaw take me aback. Embarrassed, I glance at our group, whose members have just carpooled up a rough, winding road to keep our appointment with him. My first thought is, "True, we are an hour late, but what's the big deal?"

The twenty-five of us gathered in Charleston, West Virginia, that May weekend were Christians active in environmental advocacy. Some had never seen a mountaintop removal (MTR) coal operation, the most egregious assault on God's good Earth, at least in Appalachia. On a massive scale, mountains are lopped off to expose coal, which is then scooped up and the remaining debris shoved down into valleys. The process is lucrative for coal companies, as it employs few workers and uses relatively simple equipment. Gibson and his family are holdouts, refusing to sell their land on Kayford Mountain, even though it is now surrounded by a colossal mining operation, and they have established a private foundation to help protect their home place. Our visit to the fifty-seven-acre site would provide an opportunity to see the devastation close up.

A short, middle-aged man with a barrel chest and straw-blond hair, Gibson pauses to consolidate his thoughts. Later he would tell me, "I know I sound angry, and I say things that might hurt. But look how they are annihilating the land—how can I not be angry?" Now Gibson starts talking about the churches down in the valley, how they have quietly stepped aside from confronting the destruction of mountains, water-sheds, and a culture.

"I'm glad church people have finally come," Gibson says. "But if all you are going to do is look around and then go back to your lives, you're wasting my time." Gibson is wearing an iridescent T-shirt emblazoned with his MountainKeepers logo, referring to the beleaguered, coal-lined mountains: "Love Them, Leave Them, Just Don't Destroy Them."

Gibson is undoubtedly the best known of all anti-MTR activists, having spoken at numerous universities, conferences, seminars, and demonstrations and been a significant subject in several documentary films and interviews. He does not thrive on the attention. "I wish people did not know my name. That I did not have to spend my life doing what I do [fighting MTR] but could just live up here enjoying my life."

Later that afternoon, stunned and sobered by the spectacle of mountain massacre, our group descends the dirt road back to Charleston. Christians For The Mountains is birthed. We decide that our focus will be on ending mountaintop removal. Our founding scripture is Psalm 24:I, "The Earth is the Lord's, and all that it contains." Our goal is to engage churches and their people to oppose mountaintop removal as a moral sin to repent and overcome.

Drawing on scripture, theology, and tradition is critical to successfully engage churches. Thankfully, this repository is abundant, rich, and unambiguous. The first book of the Bible begins by laying out the goodness of creation, the purpose of humanity, the problem of humans violating boundaries, and the possibility for restoration. In concise language, as recorded in Genesis 2:15–17, God gives humanity the task of helping to shape creation, the responsibility to protect it, and the privilege of being sustained by it, and admonishes us not to encroach on its limits.

The Genesis verse on dominion portrays God handing over a certain responsibility for creation to humans (1:26), analogous to parents handing over their children to school for the day. God desires humans to enhance creation. Cultivating crops such as apples, almonds, and corn; domesticating animals such as honeybees and dogs; and beautifying the Earth through flower gardens and landscaping projects are ways in which humanity has handled dominion responsibly and creatively. A key biblical term is *fruitful*, which could translate to modern parlance as "sustainable, healthy, vigorous."

Christians For The Mountains has no paid staff or office, but as we hoist our mast to the cause, wind fills our sails. With a few hundred dollars from our founding convention and a later conference, we develop a DVD project, *The Mountain Mourning Collection*, using a script template and visual materials provided by the indefatigable MTR roadshow trooper Dave Cooper. We "baptize" the project with scripture and traditional Appalachian and hymnal music and develop our basic introductory film, *Mountain Mourning*. At our urging, B. J. Gudmundsson, West Virginia Filmmaker of the Year for 2005, visits activist Maria Gunnoe and puts together a film of her story, *Look What They've Done*. Several weeks later Gudmundsson visits Larry Gibson on Kayford Mountain, tags along behind him as he shows a group around, and breaks down in tears when she sees Hells Gate, a shocking overlook onto active mountaintop removal. From this footage, shot unrehearsed in harsh lighting, Gudmundsson creates the poignant film *Keeper of the Mountains*. "My life is forever changed," says Gudmundsson, who has cut her own household energy consumption by 33 percent while becoming an ardent campaigner against the carnage of MTR.

The *Mountain Mourning Collection* is now in its third print run; generous contributions keep the DVD project afloat. Many copies are distributed free, with the stipulation that recipients share the film and its message far and wide. Our goal is simple: stir people to action by getting the message out. Our greatest inspiration comes from hearing appreciative comments from mountain folks who have long lived without hope but now see a glimmer of it.

What does it mean that the Earth belongs to God? All theistic faiths believe in a deity-created world. The Abrahamic faiths—Judaism, Christianity, and Islam—point to a transcendent Creator God who is involved and interested in creation. The Earth is God's property, so to speak. All living beings belong to God, as do the land, water, and atmospheric strata that constitute the planet. Human beings are an integral part of the global ecosystem, with a unique covenantal role to reflect the image of God.

During Memorial Day weekend 2006, almost a hundred supporters accompanied Larry Gibson on a mile-and-a-half hike to a three-acre wooded hillock. On that hill some of Gibson's ancestors lie buried in two-hundred-year-old Stover Cemetery. The property is under the control of Cantenary Coal, a subsidiary of giant Arch Coal Company. From the hilltop, barren vistas of flattened, hardpan earth stretch in all directions. The earth, too, is dead, victim of a nation's insatiable thirst for energy and the lust of companies eager for profit.

Nervous company security guards sign the walkers in. The procession is orderly, sober, tight-faced. Strains of "Amazing Grace" waft through the air, and a young woman breaks down sobbing. "I didn't know it was this bad!" she cries in outraged hurt. We reach the graves, where the land is overgrown with trees and lush undergrowth typical of the world's oldest and most botanically diverse temperate hardwood forest. The contrast to the seemingly endless wasteland that starts a few yards away is surreal.

We conduct a memorial service. Stories, prayers, and quiet reflection deepen our awareness of the meaning of our lives, our debt to past generations, and our commitment to those who will follow. We ponder the web of greed, insatiable energy addiction, and misplaced values that created this scene and is responsible for a world plunging toward a future bereft of beauty, wholeness, and ecological community. "What profit is there to gain even the whole world yet lose one's soul?" Jesus asked.

Gibson's coal-laden land might sell for millions. As our group slowly makes its way off the old burying ground, he is reflective, speaking in measured tones: "What is it in your life that is not for sale?"

Everything today seems to be a commodity with a price tag. Even arguments about mountaintop removal tend to default to the trump card of cost-benefit economics. A person like Gibson, who reveres long-gone and never-known ancestors, is an anachronism. A person who does not jump at the opportunity to escape a backwoods cabin for a comfortable suburban home is unsophisticated. A Christian minister once chastened Gibson on a panel discussion: "Larry, your country needs energy, and you have coal. Let go and get over it."

In July 2007, Cantenary Coal blasts and bulldozes a large section of the hill that holds Stover Cemetery, though regulations prohibit blasting or mining within one hundred feet of a cemetery. Horrified and shocked, Gibson reports that graves have been obliterated. Since our Memorial Day gathering, he had been seeking to restore the cemetery with volunteer and family help; graves were to be marked and recorded. Yet coal officials had continually denied access, and now, without the documented grave markers, redress would be difficult. One assumes the company made further profit in gouging coal from the mountain's split belly.

The name Jezebel is infamous because of a Bible story recorded in I Kings 21. King Ahab, Jezebel's husband, desires a neighbor's vineyard and offers to buy it for a good price. Naboth, the owner, refuses, saying, "God forbid that I would transfer my inheritance passed on by my ancestors." Not deterred, Jezebel hires hit men to falsely accuse Naboth of treason and put him to death. In following Naboth's example, Larry Gibson has endured abuse and threats.

"What the coal companies are doing is *genocide*," Gibson says. "Some people tell me I shouldn't use the word *genocide*, since people are not put to death. But our way of life is being annihilated. Doesn't that count for anything? This is genocide of the Appalachian culture."

People who believe in a God who is Creator of this planet should square with the following question: Did God create this planet so that, in order for West Virginia to have a vibrant economy, its mountains and streams have to be destroyed? Or is the problem how our economy is run?

Those of us who take guidance from the Bible must look to the ancient Hebrew prophets, such as Elijah, who faced down the idols of their time. Carbon-based energy is a paramount idol of our era, not unlike the ancient Canaanite "Baals" of fertility, prosperity, and tribal aggrandizement. Our modern energy gods promise prosperity and comfort but seduce us into a hell of social disintegration and extinction by ecocide. They demand ever-new forms of human and ecological sacrifice. But the verdant mountains, beautiful streams, and neighborly, culturally rich communities of West Virginia, eastern Kentucky, and adjacent Tennessee and Virginia now being sacrificed to the energy Molech will not satiate the monster. Each sacrifice only whets its appetite for more while further addicting its followers to the opium of fossil-fuel energy.

Is God's purpose for humanity to be summed up in our being producers and consumers? If so, then mountaintop mining is one way to keep the lights on while paying wages, stock dividends, and taxes. Or does God's purpose for us include gratitude for the beauty and wonders of the Earth, respect for its intrinsic integrity, promises kept to future generations, and humility and restraint in the face of technological hubris? If the latter is true, then an economy that incorporates these values without destroying the Earth is possible, and people of faith need to act accordingly. Some things are just not for sale.

Allen Johnson is coordinator of the steering committee for Christians For The Mountains (www.christiansforthemountains.org), a regional initiative to summon Christians and their churches to appreciate God's creation and advocate for its protection and restoration. Networking with existing religious and environmental advocacy groups, it has gained national attention through its opposition to mountaintop-removal mining.

Johnson earned an undergraduate degree in biology, but his path took a new turn after he joined a 1993 delegation to Haiti with Christian Peacemaker Teams. He became a committed advocate for eco-justice, helping to found the Evangelical Environmental Network, one of four partners of the National Religious Partnership for the Environment. On a fellowship at the Eastern Baptist Theological Seminary, he earned a master's degree in theology and public policy. He has produced a weekly local radio program on Christian faith and environmental responsibility, led outdoor spiritual retreats in several states, and serves on the steering committee of the Religious Campaign for Forest Conservation. He and his wife, Debora, live on several acres adjacent to the Monongahela National Forest in West Virginia, where he is director of the county library system.

Splitting the Sea ... So What!

Zoë Klein

Who is like you, Almighty God, who split the Sea of Reeds for our people to cross . . . ?

You split the sea. Big deal; it was one sea, one time. Such limited power; it's not even such a big sea! Let us tell you about power. You split one sea, while we, made in your divine image, have resurrected an explosion of primitive organisms in all seven seas, killing all sorts of larger species of fish. Because of our might, 90 percent of the world stocks of cod, tuna, and other big fish have vanished over the last fifty years. And we have wiped out most of the once-colorful coral reefs off our most popular coasts.

You split the Red Sea, ho hum. We've created the "red tide," our clever name for algal blooms, in which microscopic organisms (dinoflagellates) create thick masses near the ocean's surface. Don't think for a moment, however, that we have limited our palette to red—oh, no. We have nurtured great masses of phytoplankton that can turn our oceans mucus green or brown as well. You killed some Egyptians, that's all! It seems so anthropocentric. We, on the other hand, are far more varied. Our poison is not limited to humans alone; rather, seabirds, fish, marine mammals, and more are exposed to our effective neurotoxins. The gentle and graceful manatee washes up with lungs full of blood. We are affecting our planet, with its beautiful swirling cloud-swept atmosphere, like a slow-hitting meteor.

One sea! Big deal! We've knocked out 75 percent of the kelp forests off California. We've created 150 oxygen-depleted dead zones throughout the seven seas. We've increased the levels of harmful bacteria and jellyfish. Hundreds of gray whales have washed ashore dead or sick from waters we've made acidic. You split one sea. Why, just recently, under our stewardship, a twenty-five-square-mile ice shelf broke off of Canada's Arctic coast. We have megatrawlers scraping entire ecosystems off the sea floor. We have acoustic fish finders, nerve gas disposal sites, and forty-mile drift nets. We created plastic debris, pesticides, fertilizer runoff, and sewage sludge, and we have changed the basic ingredients of the ocean's living soup.

In the year the world's tallest skyscrapers fell, the world's largest floating oil rig sank off Brazil. In Ecuador, more oil has leaked into the ground than was spilled in the *Exxon Valdez* disaster; the whole land reeks of oil, and large black drops form on vegetables when it rains. When the late Saddam Hussein ordered seven hundred Kuwaiti oil wells to be set on fire, he began history's most uncontrolled experiment on the effects of air pollution. With black clouds hovering for years over the Arabian Peninsula, chemicals fusing in ways scientists could never imagine, and five hundred miles of coastline awash in oil, the Gulf War was turned into a war against the gulf. From above, NASA photographed a poisonous paisley of black and blue swirls. Rosy-hued shorebirds drawn from Africa by ancient memories pause in the fragrant marshes and intertidal flats, feathers glued, nostrils clogged, searing bright eyes entombed in asphalt.

After Cain was "cursed from the ground" for slaying his brother, he could no longer work the land that had soaked up Abel's blood; it would not yield to him (Genesis 4:11–12). So instead, Cain built the very first city (Genesis 4:17). We see his bloody fingerprints in every concrete city, amid the graffiti and violence. We are as sick as we make the world around us, no less. We are violent by nature because we are violent with nature.

We have adopted the un-Jewish belief in an unnatural heaven, a place above and beyond this world. It's a heaven that deludes us to trust that, after all the mess we make, we ascend, we get out, our souls pristine and unsoiled. We have rejected our ancient Hebrew faith that eternity is not in a separate heaven but in the promise of a future reconciliation on Earth, a return to the Garden of Eden, with our swords beat into plowshares. The oldest form of afterlife belief in Judaism is resurrection: the belief in the precious reunion of body and soul, or earth and spirit.

We were founded by a shepherd, not a carpenter. We are an agricultural religion, an oral culture of storytellers. We forgot that we are a religion of the land, our holidays agricultural. Our sages studied in the vineyards of Babylon, expounding under trees. Deborah dispensed judgment under her date palm. Shabbat ends with the appearance of three stars. We have blessings for rain, dew, thunder, rainbows. Once every twenty-eight years, we say Birkat HaChamah, an astronomical blessing over the sun. Torah is filled with instructions protecting the Earth. The majority of our laws concerning *tzedakah* (charity) are based on agriculture. Set aside a tenth of your crop (Deuteronomy 26:11–12). Do not harvest the corners of your field; leave what remains for the poor (Leviticus 19:9). Do not destroy fruit trees in times of war (Deuteronomy 20:19). The menorah is patterned after a plant. The Torah is the tree of life.

The Hebrew root for "spirit," *n'shamah*, is the same as that for "wind," *n'shimah*. The kabbalists say that the forgotten pronunciation of the name of our God is *Yah* on the whispered in-breath and *Weh* on the whispered out-breath. Thus the whole name of God is formed by a single cycle of the breath, the awesome mystery of God's name not separate from the mystery of breathing.

You made us very powerful when you said that you created the world for our sake (Genesis 1:26–29). You made us powerful enough to ignore your plea: "See to it that you do not spoil and destroy My world—for if you do, there will be no one else to repair it" (Kohelet Rabbah 7:28).

In your love for us, you split one sea to redeem one people, our people, and we've churned and corrupted all seven seas for our love of nothing but ourselves. Who is like you, Almighty God, who limits your immeasurable power by *only* splitting the Sea of Reeds!

Rabbi Zoë Klein is senior rabbi at Temple Isaiah in Los Angeles. She pursued the rabbinate out of a passion for ancient texts, mythology, liturgy, and poetry. As an author, Klein has been published in Harper's Bazaar, Tikkun, Jewish Journal, *and* Torat Hayim, *and she has written poems and prayers used in houses of prayer around the country. A book of her poetry,* House Plant Meadow, *will be published by David R. Godine, and her novel* The Prophet *is slated to be published by Simon & Schuster in 2009. Klein appeared in* Glamour *magazine in December 2002 in a feature on women of the cloth. She gives numerous presentations each year and has been a panel participant or keynote speaker at various assemblies all over the country. She also has appeared as a commentator on the History Channel program* Digging for the Truth.

Finding Communion
with Creation

Mark MacDonald

"It was early in the morning. . . ." Like many other congregations on that Easter Sunday, we heard the beginning of the story of Jesus's rising from the dead. But I was reading it in Navajo to a gathering of elders and young people in the middle of Navajo Nation. As I spoke, the oldest person there, an elder who understood no English, said loudly (in Navajo), "Yes!"

It seemed a little early in the narrative for this much enthusiasm, so I assumed I had made a mistake—something that happens often in my pronunciation of Navajo. So I said it again. This time the *yes* was even louder and more enthusiastic.

After Communion, I asked our lay pastor if I had pronounced the words correctly. With surprise on her face, she said, "Of course." Pressing her further, I asked what Shima' ("my mother," a way of respectfully describing and greeting older women in Navajo) was so excited about. She explained,

"The early dawn is the most important part of the day to her. Father Sky and Mother Earth meet at that time and produce all that is necessary for life. It is the holiest time of the day. Jesus would pick that good time of day to be raised."

The early dawn is certainly the best time for new life, though I had never thought of it in this connection. In most biblical narratives the time of day seemed trivial, given, I imagined, simply to make the story more vivid. I had never considered, at least in this context, that an observation about the physical world could be theologically and spiritually revealing, that it suggested a communion between God, humanity, and creation that is fundamental to our moral, spiritual, and physical existence.

It took me a while to absorb this. An elder with no formal schooling had repositioned the central narrative of my life firmly within the physical world and all its forces and interactions. It was an ecological reading of a story that, for me, had been trapped inside a flat virtual world misnamed "spiritual." Shima' had opened a door to a world radically new but recognizably old—one undeniably closer to the world of Jesus than to the Christianity of my cultural and institutional training. She had uncovered in a familiar tale a primal, long-ignored layer of spiritual consciousness that was also an ecological consciousness.

This observation by Shima' stays close to me, even years later. And I have come to believe that it poses a critical challenge to a much larger audience. It points to a prophetic confrontation with the imperial and materialistic cosmology of the West.

We perceive that the rapidly globalizing society of business and development has lost its way to a livable future for humanity and for the larger community of creation. Our modern cosmology can describe, calculate, and commodify in amazing detail and with relentless breadth. Yet it apparently lacks the power to inspire the world's communal moral imagination toward sufficient concern and effective action. Whatever the positive aspects of our culture of commerce, it shows very little capacity to understand the life-giving interconnectedness of creation.

It has been my privilege and honor to participate in issues that involve the interaction of indigenous peoples' rights and environmental protection, especially with regard to the Arctic National Wildlife Refuge. In these controversies, it has become evident that the moral and spiritual pivot is found in the living relationship between indigenous communities and their ecological matrix. The lack of imagination displayed by the dominant society in its approach to these vital issues is stunning.

The weight of evidence is clear: most people, including many environmentalists, do not understand the living, symbiotic relationship that indigenous peoples have with this Earth. It is also painfully clear that many individuals, governments, and cultures do not understand their own living relationship with their environment. Although some pay homage to the idea of "wild places," even this growing appreciation fails to identify what is at stake. We live in a world that may be analyzed, measured, and described with amazing sophistication and intricacy, but its meaning and value have been lost.

If the truth be told or, perhaps more accurately, if the truth be honored, the place of human beings in the world we inhabit is morally absolute. To treat our environment well is not just a good idea. It is the only idea. For this world, by its design (whether or not you believe in a Creator), is what humanizes us. Without it there may be blood pumping in our hearts and oxygen processed in our lungs, but we will clearly be less than human.

Our current environmental crisis has revealed the huge deficits in how we understand our relationship to the place where we live. For most people, this relationship has been reduced to a chemical, mechanical, and economic exchange that can be reproduced in other places and in other ways. We may recognize the re-creative and regenerative value of wild places, but we tend to see it as an economic function. More fundamentally, we seem to have forgotten how this world, as made, has shaped and formed us. Our cosmology has overlooked vital aspects of our existence; we seem to believe that there can be human life apart from the world in which God placed us. Our actions, following from this idolatrous and anthropocentric myth, threaten us at every turn.

Western Christianity has rightly received criticism for some of its unhelpful contributions to our separation from the physical world. Yet I suggest, inspired by Shima', that what we endure is a reading of our scriptures that is shaped and limited by our cosmology. I am not criticizing the conclusions or methods of science, or our techniques for the study of scripture. I am only identifying their limitations in inspiring the moral imagination of a world in crisis. These disciplines do not adequately describe the comprehensive moral community we share with the rest of creation. Nor is an adequate account of the cosmology available at the root of Christian theology. (This is something we often find highlighted by Eastern Orthodox commentators on ecological issues.)

It is critical, therefore, that the globalizing West reread some of its central cultural narratives—and not just its biblical texts—with a wider imaginative lens. First Nations, the People of the Land, suggest, by their very relationship to other nations, that there is an ecological "reading" of what it means to be human, what it means to be a people, and what it means to be faithful to the Creator of all that is. The response of Shima' to the Easter story is just one such rereading. The stubborn resistance of the People of the Land is an inspiration. They will not accept a definition of their humanity that does not include an ecological and spiritual accounting of their relationship to the land.

Western religious groups have demanded that indigenous peoples accept modern cosmology as a prerequisite to being received and assimilated into the institutional life of churches. But even among the most assimilated and church-related

Native people, this cosmology has had little or no apparent traction. Such resistance is intriguing and underlines their sophistication in these matters. It also hints at overlooked connections between indigenous cosmologies and the narratives they hear in scripture.

Water, for example, holds a rich cosmological significance for Native people of the dry Southwest and for the early followers of Jesus. Both the Old and New Testaments are rich in images, symbolic meanings, and references to water as it was experienced in the environment—its presence and the lack of it. In the culminating event of Jesus's baptism by John in the Jordan River, water becomes the interpretive lens through which the web of life—humanity, creation, and Creator—are perceived and understood. In other Gospel events as well, such as Jesus calming or walking on the sea, bringing forth loaves and fishes, and healing the lame man by the pool of Bethesda, creation is revealed through water as the supportive and ever-present web of moral, spiritual, and physical life.

In developed societies, our relationship with the physical world is no longer defined by the mutuality, personalism, and intimacy of earlier traditions. Indigenous peoples have suffered from holding this position in the face of intense, persistent, and almost universal opposition. Indeed, they have been compelled to abandon their position as a condition of receiving the benefits of modern life, even as the Native view is receiving late and timid approval from Western science.

The relationships we must seek within the web of life are best summarized as communion. Communion, which is animated by and joined in the divine love of the Creator, is intimate, like the relationship of mother to child. It is multifaceted and complex, ineffable like the divine being that made it. Though such communion with creation we gain life, a life shaped and guided by ecological awareness and morality and the practice of ecological partnership.

I have a Native friend who says that, for the People of the Land, wholeness can take place only "on the land." To be on the land, as he describes it, is to be in any place that gives the sense of what I have called the communion of creation. He applies this insight to healing, education, and service, insisting, for instance, that theological education must take place on the land. Growing in understanding and appreciation of this insight, I have come to believe that it applies to how we live in the largest sense. "The land" need not be an officially wild place; it can be any piece of physical or spiritual geography that helps us understand and reenter the communion that is ours as children of God's creation. We must go on the land to be healed and to find our way to a livable future.

The Right Reverend Mark MacDonald *was appointed the National Indigenous Anglican Bishop of Canada in January 2007. Previously he was consecrated as bishop of Alaska in 1997, and in 2006 he was appointed*

as the pastoral bishop of the Episcopal Church of Navajoland, a position he continues to hold. Bishop MacDonald has had a long and varied ministry, holding positions in Mississauga, Ontario; Duluth, Minnesota; Tomah and Mauston, Wisconsin; Portland, Oregon; and the Southeast Regional mission of the diocese of Navajoland.

Presently the bishop is on the boards of the Indigenous Theological Training Institute and New Directions, and is the board chair for Church Innovations, a member of the Episcopal Council of Indian Ministries. He is also a Third Order Franciscan. Among his published works are Native American Youth Ministries, coauthored with Dr. Carol Hampton, and A Strategy for Growth for the Episcopal Church: Joining Multiculturalism and Evangelism. *He was editor for Liturgical Studies IV,* The Chant of Life: Inculturation and the People of the Land *(New York: Church Publishing, 2003).*

The Road Back to Paradise

Ingrid Mattson

The Saint Lawrence River is nineteen hundred miles long. Its wide mouth empties the river's flow into the Atlantic Ocean, where whales and majestic icebergs drift throughout the summer months. The river begins more modestly where the northern and southern shores of Lake Ontario curve toward each other, channeling the cold waters of the Great Lakes into the riverbed.

My siblings and I were born on the Canadian side of the river, but the island we lived on was closer to New York State. This area is now called the Thousand Islands, but before there was a Canada, and before there was an America, the indigenous people—the Iroquois—called it "the garden of the Great Spirit." So I guess my six brothers and sisters and I grew up in *jennah*— the "garden" that the Qur'an describes as the spiritual home of all people. We played in thick woods of maple and hickory, hiked across fields of long grass, chicory, and thistles looking for raspberry and blackberry bushes, and roamed along the shore searching for salamanders and crayfish.

It really was beautiful. But we were, after all, children of Adam, and, as the angels feared in the Qur'anic creation story (they said to God, "Will you place on the earth one who will ruin it and shed blood there?"), we would make a mess of many things. To begin with, there was the question of those indigenous people. As children, my siblings and I spent long July afternoons on the edge of the forest digging for their arrowheads, flints, and pottery shards. Where had the people gone? No one thought to talk about this Cain and Abel story.

Then there was the question of what we later residents did to the river itself. Flowing over deep layers of limestone, refreshed with generous rain and snow every year, the river seemed impervious to anything we might throw its way. And we did throw many things its way. In fact, because our island lacked refuse collection services, it seemed easiest to let the current take our trash away. I don't know where all our tin cans and plastic wrappers ended up, but the consequences of some of our ignorant acts seem clear. Once we deliberately sank an old car in a nearby bay to create a good fishing hole. Little wonder that our own children, wanting to enjoy the same sort of fun their parents had during summer holidays on the island, now catch only a few small perch and a rare, undersized bass in a day spent fishing.

The truth is that we did not realize, back in the 1960s, that we were damaging the river, killing plant and animal life, and poisoning others and ourselves. But as years passed and we were exposed to more information about the environment, we became appalled at our earlier behavior. We had, after all, been taught that it is wrong to damage property and harm others. We had internalized the principles; we simply were not aware of the negative consequences of our actions in this respect.

And so, as we grew into adulthood and opportunities arose, some of us planted trees and others cleaned up polluted sites, or gave money to save the rain forests, or took up organic gardening. By this time we had scattered across the country and even the world, and we took these actions in our new communities. But the river—our river—always called us back. We wanted to be there and to make it better, and that would mean living and working together for at least part of the year.

This would not be easy, for the years had witnessed other changes in us. By the time we became aware of our need to relate to the river in a new way, we had taken different spiritual paths. Certainly the Muslim in the family (me) found ample proof in Islam that she had an obligation to respect and conserve the environment. The Christians, Jews, and secular humanists among us found their own proofs for similar, if not identical, obligations. But there were many other things we did not agree about. In fact, at times we had serious disagreements.

This is my story. It is also the human story. Muslims believe that the children of Adam do not inherit sin from their ancestors. But we do inherit the good that our ancestors have bequeathed to us, and we are burdened with repairing what they have damaged. In our time, in every place where Muslims live—whether they are the majority or the minority—serious societal problems exist that must be addressed. The environment must be protected or restored; indigenous and other minority groups must be relieved of the burden of years of systematic injustice; children and the poor need daily support and meaningful opportunities for advancement.

The Prophet Muhammad, may God's peace and blessings be upon him, told his companions that "there will come a time when the best property of a Muslim will be the sheep he takes to the mountain peaks and watered lands, fleeing with his religion from tribulation." But such flight is a last resort, to be taken only when it is impossible to hold on to one's faith while remaining in society. Muslims have lived through times when this was the only option. But sooner or later they came back down the mountains and started the hard work of living and rebuilding together with other people. Key questions now for our community are: when are we obliged to work with non-Muslims to build a better society, and when are we obliged to limit our work to whatever we can accomplish on our own?

Clearly, there is no simple answer—despite the claims of those who confuse isolation with piety and those who confuse every ease with goodness. Not every alliance between Muslims and non-Muslims is bad, nor is every alliance good. In trying to distinguish the good from the bad, we need both accurate facts and a sound methodology for applying the most appropriate rules to those facts. Let us begin with the rules.

Over the centuries, Muslim scholars developed a number of useful models for organizing and prioritizing needs and responsibilities. One of these models identifies the five interests that Islamic law aims to protect: religion, life, property, intellect, and family. Within each category, interests are prioritized according to three degrees of necessity (that is, essential, important, and desirable). So, for example, it is desirable to sit quietly and read some of the Qur'an every day, but it is essential to pray the five ritual prayers at the designated times. In the interest of protecting religion, we cannot neglect something that is essential for something that is merely desirable. Similarly, it is desirable to regularly engage in intelligent conversation, but it is essential to preserve reverence for God. Thus it is not permitted for a Muslim to maintain a close friendship with a highly intelligent person who engages him or her in stimulating conversation, if that person continuously derides the sacred (Qur'an 5:57–58). Indeed, since preserving faith is the highest priority, it is important that Muslims avoid demoralizing dependence on other faith communities for their protection and material needs.

Getting the facts straight, as I have mentioned, is also essential for deciding if a particular action is praiseworthy or to be avoided. Consider, for example, participation in rallies or demonstrations. In some cases the message conveyed by the organizers of such rallies is very different from that of the participants. The organizers may be promoting an antistate (or anarchist) message, while some participants intend to protest only a particular unjust policy of the state. Muslims must ensure that they are not simply swelling the ranks of groups whose message they essentially do not support.

But if it is truly injustice that is being protested or justice that is being promoted, how do Muslims weigh the merit of their participation in alliances and coalitions with others? Here, the Islamic legal distinction between a personal obligation (*fard 'ayn*) and a collective obligation (*fard kifayah*) is useful. In the classical tradition, this distinction was applied to obligations within the Muslim community. Each Muslim, for example, is personally obliged to feed, shelter, and protect his or her own offspring and needy adult relatives. It is the responsibility of the whole community, however, to ensure that foundlings, orphans, and poor children are also cherished and nourished. Normally the state bears ultimate responsibility for this obligation, but in the absence of a well-functioning state, the Muslim community is not relieved of its obligation. If the Muslim community does not work to develop social structures and institutions to care for needy children within its midst, all members of the community will bear the burden of sinful neglect.

Many Muslim communities in America have recognized this responsibility and have established soup kitchens and community welfare programs. But even if every mosque in America operated a full range of social service programs, the effect on society at large would be minimal. Similarly, even if every mosque in America were a model of energy conservation, American cities would still be filled with thousands of children suffering from debilitating asthma due to air pollution. Unless Muslims bring to the public sphere their beliefs about distributive justice, environmental stewardship, and other good causes, our activities will remain marginal.

In this age of globalization and transnationalism, we must recognize the imperative to extend the notion of communal obligation beyond the Muslim community. Our most natural allies in shaping public policy are those who share many of our core beliefs and values, and we can work with them as long as they are respectful of our faith and practices. Clearly there are groups, both secular and religious, who are so hostile to Muslims that we should not join with them even in shared concerns, lest we lend any credibility to their organizations. Within the communities that give rise to those groups, however, are many others eager to work respectfully with Muslims to further just causes. Only an ignorant person would believe that Muslims have a monopoly on caring for justice or for God's creation. The Prophet Muhammad even praised the pre-Islamic Arab polytheists for having furthered the cause of justice in the Pact of al-Fudul. Justice has been the cause of all God's prophets, and God has placed love of justice in the hearts of his servants.

Those who are "upright," those who "stand up for justice" (Qur'an 57:25), form an axis of goodness around which communities of faith can and must come together. There is no road back to paradise, except the one we build with God's grace and with our good deeds in this life. In his infinite wisdom and mercy, God has placed us in a time and place in which Muslims, Christians, Jews, and others find that our essential interests are inevitably intertwined. We can choose to ignore each other, and so limit our ability to lay a path of good deeds, or we can unite when needed around an axis of goodness and justice.

Dr. Ingrid Mattson is director of the Islamic chaplaincy and professor at the Macdonald Center for Islamic Studies and Christian-Muslim Relations at Hartford Seminary in Hartford, Connecticut. She earned her PhD in Islamic studies from the University of Chicago in 1999. Her research is focused on Islamic law and society; among her articles are studies on slavery, poverty, and Islamic legal theory. Dr. Mattson was born in Canada, and she studied philosophy at the University of Waterloo, Ontario. From 1987 to 1988 she lived in Pakistan, where she worked with Afghan refugee women. In 2006 Dr. Mattson was elected president of the Islamic Society of North America—the first convert to Islam, and the first woman, to lead the organization.

This Good Earth

Brian McLaren

We thank you, Lord, for this good Earth.

In the beginning, you created the heavens and the Earth, and you said that all creation was filled with goodness, beginning with the goodness of light. We thank you, Lord, for sun and moon and stars, for sunrises and clear days and bright, moonlit nights. We also thank you, Lord, for the gift of night—for time to rest, to sleep, to dream. And so we sing. . . .

We thank you, Lord, for continents in their slow journeys, for mountains that rise and rains that erode them grain by grain to the sea. For prairies and rolling hills, for beaches and deserts, for woodlands and glaciers, for rain forests and tundra, we thank you, for all are filled with goodness. And we thank you, Lord, for springs and streams, for marshes and estuaries, for rivers and bays, for seas and the great oceans.

For the precious gifts of soil and water and air, without which we could not live, we thank you, Lord. And so we sing. . . .*

We thank you for the wonder of life, Lord, for the grandeur hidden in a single living cell, for the marvel of DNA, for the amazing processes of respiration, digestion, reproduction, growth, and adaptation. How amazing are your creatures, Lord—the field mouse that hides in tall grasses, the gray whale that rises in the ocean, the swallows that soar and dive above the surface of a still pond, the tiny red eft that lives so quietly in the forest, the salmon that fights currents to return to the stream of its origin, the gorillas and elephants and giraffes, the butterflies and dragonflies and ants. We thank you for beloved dogs and cats and other companion creatures who become part of our lives. And so we sing. . . .

But Lord, we cannot only thank you. We must also confess to you our sin in failing to honor and care for your beautiful and good creation. How many precious and irreplaceable species have gone extinct because of our greedy rush to make money, our ignorant slowness to understand the intricate balance of your works, our prideful and careless desire to act not as stewards of your world but as its heartless slave masters and selfish

* For use in public worship, readers can recite the prayer, and the congregation can chant the refrain on a single tone (A is recommended, with harmonies if desired). On the word *Earth*, voices rise a whole step (to B) and then return to the original note. If musicians wish to add musical accompaniment to the refrain, they would play A major and at *Earth* would play B minor, then return to A major. They also could sustain B minor through the recited prayer.

tyrants. Air, soil, and water show ugly symptoms of our own inner pollution; they suffer because of the greed, arrogance, lust, ignorance, and hate that pollute our hearts and cultures. We are sorry, Creator, for our offenses to your creation, and we wish to stop polluting, defacing, and destroying your world. Instead, we wish to care for, protect, love, preserve, and appreciate your beautiful and manifold works, and so we sing. . . .

We thank you, God, for speaking to our world through Jesus. He told us that, just as you care for every sparrow, you care for us. He reminded us that you give the wildflowers their natural beauty and you wish to clothe us with beauty in a similar way. He taught us that wisdom is hidden in the growth of the smallest seed, in the turning of seasons, in every corner of your amazing creation. He taught us to see every creature as beloved by you, God our Creator, and he called us to live with your love pulsing in our hearts. So let us learn to see and love this good Earth as Jesus did, and to care for it and enjoy it and rejoice in it, so that the Earth may indeed be filled with the glory of God as the waters cover the sea. And so we sing. . . .

And we sing again. . . .

And we sing again.

Amen.

Brian McLaren *(brianmclaren.net) is a best-selling author, speaker, and pastor who networks with Christians around the world for constructive engagement with global crises. He previously worked as a college English instructor and then, for twenty-four years, as a pastor in the Washington, D.C., area, at Cedar Ridge Community Church (crcc.org). His books A New Kind of Christian, A Generous Orthodoxy, and Everything Must Change have played a key role in the formation of an international movement called "the emerging church." He serves as board chair for Sojourners (sojo.net), whose mission is to articulate the biblical call to social justice, and is active in the organization Emergent Village (emergentvillage.com), which fosters connections among missional Christians. McLaren is a leader in affirming the spiritual dimensions of the environmental movement, economic justice, and peace making. Time magazine named him one of America's twenty-five most influential Evangelicals, describing him as a "paradigm shifter" capable of bringing liberals and conservatives together. He loves the outdoors and has a special interest in wildlife.*

Restoring the Inner Landscape

Seyyed Hossein Nasr

My childhood was spent in my country of birth, Iran, with its magnificent mountains, deserts, forests, and seashores. During the early years of my life, my family usually spent the summer in the foothills of Mount Damavand, not far from Tehran. This is the highest mountain peak in Asia west of the Hindu Kush. There and in other places I visited in early childhood, I was able to experience the beauty and majesty of nature. So by the time I came to America at the age of twelve, I had already developed great love for and intimacy with nature untouched by human hands.

In the United States I had the privilege of visiting some of the most beautiful natural sites from Cape Cod to Sequoia National Park. I even spent a whole summer in California's Sierra Nevada and another summer inside Rocky Mountain National Park in Colorado.

In 1950 I went to the Massachusetts Institute of Technology to study physics while continuing to explore the natural areas of New England. The contrast of New Hampshire's beautiful mountains, the fall foliage of Vermont and western Massachusetts, and the rocky coast of Maine with the ugly, industrialized part of Cambridge around MIT and the drab ambience of many of the school buildings left a painful mark upon my mind and soul. I could not simply ignore this contrast. And when I read Rachel Carson's description of polluted streams in her book *Silent Spring*, it confirmed what I was experiencing. I felt, however, that something much deeper than science was at the root of the problem.

An event that brought home to me the reality of a widespread environmental crisis was the construction of Route 128, the beltway around Boston. I lived with my family in Arlington Heights, a town between Cambridge and Concord, and many animals from the forests around Concord, such as deer, would come near our home. But after the highway was built, we were suddenly cut off from the natural ambience of the hinterland, and the neighborhood ecology began to change. This loss left a deep impression upon me. I came to understand in a vivid and palpable way that a major disaster was on the horizon.

Having been endowed with a philosophical mind, I sought to discover the real causes of this crisis, beyond bad environmental planning or poor engineering. I brought to my inquiry my studies at MIT and later at Harvard, which had given me a solid grounding in several disciplines: modern Western science (both physics and geology); the history of Western philosophy and the history of science; Western Christianity; and non-Western traditions and their philosophies of nature. I was also blessed with the ability to read several languages and make use of original sources in those languages.

In my doctoral thesis and in other early work, I had argued that modern science—based on its mechanistic view of the cosmos—leads to the alienation of human beings from nature as a sacred and spiritual reality, and that this approach is not the only possible science of nature. Other paradigms have served as frameworks for other sciences of nature—especially those of Islam, the school of traditional science I knew best.

The final impetus to assemble and communicate these ideas came from an invitation to deliver the Rockefeller Series Lectures at the University of Chicago in 1966. All the elements from my personal and academic background came together in the course of this work. The text of those lectures appeared two years later as a book titled *The Encounter of Man and Nature: The Spiritual Crisis of Modern Man*. In later editions the title was (and is still) abbreviated as *Man and Nature*, and the book continues to have readers in many languages, Prince Charles of Great Britain and Al Gore among them. It has been read in Brazil and France, by Persians and Turks as well as

Indians and Malays, and has played a humble role in awakening the Islamic world to the reality of the environmental crisis.

In the forty years since *Man and Nature* was first published, I have participated in numerous conferences on the environment and had the honor of being a keynote speaker at the first Earth Day gathering, held in Stockholm in 1971. I played a small part in founding the national park system in Iran, one of the first in Asia, and I have taught a course on man and nature at George Washington University for the past quarter century.

Over the decades I have become more and more convinced that the roots of the environmental crisis are spiritual and intellectual. This crisis must be seen as the external manifestation of a universal pollution that has turned the inner landscape of so many modern men and women from a luxuriant garden into an arid desert. Without a change of worldview and a transformation of vision, all efforts to resolve the crisis are little more than cosmetic. They can at best buy a little more time for humankind to change its vision concerning the natural world and its manner of living in and dealing with that world and the creatures that inhabit it.

Professor Seyyed Hossein Nasr is one of the world's leading experts on Islamic science and spirituality and the author of numerous books, including Man and Nature: The Spiritual Crisis of Modern Man *(1998),* Religion and the Order of Nature *(1996), and* Knowledge and the

Sacred *(1989)*. Born in Tehran, he was educated in Iran and the United States, graduating from the Massachusetts Institute of Technology and Harvard University. He returned to Iran in 1958 and was a professor at Tehran University until 1979. In addition, he served as dean of the Faculty of Letters, vice chancellor, and chancellor of Aryamehr University, and he founded the Iranian Academy of Philosophy and served as its first president. Since 1984, Dr. Nasr has been University Professor of Islamic Studies at George Washington University in Washington, D.C., and president of the Foundation for Traditional Studies. His works have been translated into many languages, including German, Spanish, Bosnian, Turkish, and Urdu.

Hippos Called My Name

David Radcliff

"El tigre! El tigre!" I'd heard excitement in Delio's voice before, when he spotted a sloth or a caiman or a troop of monkeys, but never like this. And it came through loud and clear, even though he said it in nearly a whisper—the jaguar was swimming across the river just six feet ahead of our boat. It all happened quickly, within the space of perhaps ten seconds— the sleek, muscled, gold and black creature paddling through the water, climbing the bank a few yards away, shaking off, casting a glance our way, then disappearing into the jungle.

Our New Community Project delegations to the Amazon are bent on learning about the impacts of oil drilling, cattle ranching, poverty, and international policies on this fast-retreating rain forest. But we also go to soak in the ecosystem under the tutelage of Delio, a Siona shaman and our guide. So we always head into the heart of the Cuyabeno Ecological

Reserve with high hopes of seeing pink river dolphins, a few caiman, some big-billed, small-bodied toucans flying overhead—and maybe a poison dart frog. We try not to set our sights too high, however, as on the likes of tapirs, anacondas, or especially jaguars. These are too rare to be expected in our line of sight, even if at times we may be in theirs. Delio has lived his entire fifty-two years in this part of the rain forest along the banks of the Cuyabeno River, one of the tributaries of the mighty Amazon. After the jaguar encounter, he told us he had seen the elusive creature only twice before.

This episode was sandwiched between other striking animal encounters I've had this year. In Sudan, the purpose of our delegation was to observe not wildlife but the harsh life still endured by countless communities in the southern part of that country. The war between Sudan's north and south is over, but the misery is not. We were there to chronicle and then respond to these realities.

One day, however, we took a break to travel to the shores of the Nile River just outside the village of Nimule. There's a "national park" there, although it's a park more in name than anything else; no signs demark its boundaries, and one expects to encounter no other visitors. But we weren't the only ones there. Our AK-47-toting escort knew where to find them—a herd of elephants on the far side of the stream, browsing among the trees. Then, in the foreground, sets of hooded eyes broke the surface of an eddy in the Nile—

a submerged cluster of four . . . six . . . eight hippos! We'd all seen larger mammals in our own national parks or sanctuaries elsewhere, but there was something about this encounter that made us feel as if these creatures were truly in the wild, not in a sanctuary of any kind. It was a raw, unrehearsed moment of seeing massive creatures in their element and unperturbed by a Land Rover full of shutter-snapping interlopers.

Then just a week ago (as I write this), our group was exploring a scenic gorge of the Savage River inside Denali National Park. I decided to head up the steep side of the valley in search of blueberries for the next morning's pancakes, having found some there the year before. What I found instead, as I came around the top of a jagged outcropping a few hundred feet up, was a honey-brown lynx. It had been on the opposite side of the rocks, heard me coming, and decided to exit, stage right. Our eyes met for perhaps five seconds as it crossed a grassy area about fifteen feet away—then it was gone, even though I resorted to making wounded rabbit sounds (which I'm sure sounded more wounded than rabbit) in an attempt to lure it back.

Like its much larger cousin in the Amazon, this shy feline is elusive; it usually appears in vain on the Denali visitor's must-see list. And my brief encounter wasn't the end of animal sightings in Denali—our group also had close encounters with a young bull caribou by a stream near our campsite and with a large Dall sheep ram on the misty top of Mount Margaret.

Each of these sightings in the wild was a jaw-dropping, awe-inspiring moment in its own right. Taken together, they've had the effect of a sign. I began to feel as if I'd had more than just a sequence of exceptional experiences: it felt like a call. And as I've thought more about it, it feels like a call to speak on behalf of those who have no voice—the nonhuman part of God's creation.

Certainly creation as a whole has a voice of sorts. It will respond in its own way in its own time to our abuses. The global climate, for instance, is beginning to play the hand it has been dealt by humanity. "I am warming, hear me roar" might be its theme—and the chorus won't be pretty, for human or beast. And the smallest creatures, those seen as invaders amid our amber waves of grain, are rapidly leapfrogging our latest chemical weapons. Sweet revenge, from an insect's-eye vantage point.

But for the average species, be it flora or fauna, the waves of human assaults are coming too fast and furious to either fight or flee, and many will perish. Up to a quarter of all species, plant and animal, will be gone by midcentury, some say. By the end of the century, says biologist E. O. Wilson, we'll be entering the time "of great loneliness": we'll have realized too late how much damage we've caused and how great the species losses have been. We will find ourselves more and more alone in a homogenized world, without the company of polar bears or many amphibians or coral reefs or African apes.

Will these creatures—part of God's dream for this world, so wonderfully reflective of the Creator's creativity—go quietly into the night, with no voice raised on their behalf? Or will those who have the ability speak? And will they back up their words with exemplary actions—the kind of broad-based actions that could yet prove the lifeline needed by our earthly neighbors?

At the heart of my understanding of the life and teachings of Jesus is a call to advocacy for those at the margins of society. In Jesus's time, these included women, children, people called "sinners" by religious elites, people of non-Jewish religious persuasion, and the poor.

Jesus was brazen in his concern for and actions on behalf of the marginalized. Indeed, this is largely what brought him grief, not only from the religious authorities but even from his closest followers, whom we see aghast that he might be speaking with women, welcoming children, or condemning the rich. And, of course, this behavior eventually brought him to the cross, for defying powerful institutions that sought domination and control.

Although it's not as clearly stated in terms of advocacy, it is clear that Jesus held the natural world in high regard. He often used nature as a model for human behavior, as when he instructed us to take our cue from the "birds of the air" when we fret over material desires. He sought solitude in the wilderness, retreating there to regain his bearings and energy. And he often cautioned against becoming obsessed with material wealth at the peril of our souls—a warning we might see as directed more to our hyperconsumptive times than to his.

Were Jesus speaking today, it's hard to imagine that he wouldn't have warned also about what our appetites are doing to the Earth, to its living things, and to our human companions on the planet. Each of these in its own way is voiceless—the Earth can only respond to our excesses; our poor neighbors will only suffer the coming storm as the Earth's bounty diminishes and trusted natural systems come unglued. Jesus would certainly have been their advocates.

In his absence, we must take up the call. Christians and those from other traditions have an opportunity to follow in Jesus's footsteps and the footsteps of other prophets to raise a voice for those without one. We do it by reminding each other of God's creatorship, of our scriptures' unremitting mandates to "till and keep," of the rejection of materialism by Jesus and every tradition, of the scriptural call to justice—a call mocked by global warming and the emptying of seas and water tables and arable soil and forestlands on a planet of growing population. And what of generational justice—the inheritance of life and diversity we do or don't pass on to our children?

I felt the jaguar and lynx and hippos calling my name. I am trying to respond. I've given up my car for a bicycle. Don't eat meat or shrimp. Make early morning trash-day raids through the neighbors' garbage for recyclables. Take groups abroad to experience the beauty and exigencies of God's Earth. Speak to schools, churches, colleges, clubs, or any place that will have me. Promote reforestation projects in Latin America and Africa. Turn out Web and print resources like nobody's business. Remind folks of eco-saints like Saint Francis and the youth group who washed dishes to keep their congregation from going to styrofoam. Remind myself to be open to going where these creatures may yet be calling me—places I have not had the courage or conscience to explore. And remind all of us of God's propensity to use seemingly insignificant people acting with conviction and compassion to do things we could not have imagined—in fact, that's the only way God really works.

These creatures are calling your name, too. Listen if you dare, because when you hear, you'll be pushed to make the choice that always faced our Lord—speak or be silent. Speak, and they'll question your reason and your religion. Be silent and . . . well, prepare for the time of great silence, when the growls and grunts and gestures of our earthly neighbors will be no more. And we all will be the poorer for it.

David Radcliff is director of the New Community Project, based in Elgin, Illinois (www.newcommunityproject.org). This faith-based nonprofit is working for peace through justice, care for creation, and experiential learning. Radcliff speaks at schools, colleges, churches, youth events, and community groups and leads learning tours to the Arctic, Amazon, Burma, Nepal, Sudan, Iraq, and Central America.

The Baptized Life

Larry Rasmussen

Here is Paul's word to us in 2 Corinthians 5:17: "When any-one is united to Christ, there is a new world; the old order has gone, and a new order has already begun."

Ours is a thrilling, dangerous moment for the baptized life. We stand, a bit off balance, at two tipping points. The "great transformation" (to use Karl Polanyi's term) of Earth-human relations that was set in motion with the fossil-fuel avalanche of the Industrial Revolution created the first tipping point. This shift pitted the big human economy against the great economy of creation, transporting generation upon gen-eration from "an organic, ever-renewing, land-based economy to an extractive, non-renewing, industrial economy," as Thomas Berry writes—the economy now reigning on the planet. While some of the human world grew rich beyond imagining, the biosphere and atmosphere were fatefully altered. Stored energy in the form of fossil fuels meant that great numbers of humans no longer had to live in sync with the rhythms and requirements of the renewables—with solar and hydrological cycles—or with the imperatives of fickle seasons, lazy flora, and unimproved fauna. Stored energy let us conjure up a built environment and limit our more immediate dependence upon the unbuilt environment, or so we thought. "City" replaced "country," and "organization" displaced "nature," as our environment, our habitat, our home.

The churches' ministries tagged along, as though on a leash. How many of your ministries are *not* carbon-based? How many are automobile-free, air-conditioner-free, and fast-food-free? How many of your churches have *not* moved all sacred space indoors? And, clergy, your ordination vows did not include "Before God and this community, I pledge myself to a fossil-fuel ministry," but that's the pledge you made.

Thomas Edison once chatted up Henry Ford and Harvey Firestone, and this is what Edison said: "I'd put my money on the sun and solar energy. What a source of power! I hope we don't have to wait until oil and coal run out before we tackle that." Ford and Firestone (that is, cars and tires, tailpipes and smokestacks) were admittedly a poor choice of audience. Edison badly underestimated what oil, coal, and natural gas made possible that the sun did not. None, including Edison, could resist the fossil-fuel interlude.

But now we are at a fateful moment when small changes

can make vast differences and predictable processes give way to unpredictable, nonlinear outcomes. Let liquid become a couple of degrees warmer, and it turns to steam; a couple of degrees cooler, and it turns to ice—though all the while we thought our ministries would never leave the liquid state of our baptisms. Now the downside of fossil fuels is way up, and we are, of hard necessity, at another tipping point, poised for an ecological reformation, a leap of human ingenuity, and a spiritual shift that effect a *counter*–tipping point—a tip toward Earth-honoring faith rather than Earth-abusing faith.

And who are we, the baptized, in this thrilling and dangerous moment? 'Fess up: we are Joseph the dreamer, and we are rebuked by the brothers who say, "Here comes [the] dreamer" again (Genesis 37:19). Moreover, we find ourselves dreaming in Egypt, where we, too, may well be prospering in Pharaoh's court, or trying to do so, happily seduced by the glitter and glamour of evil and fortune. Yet "way down in Egypt Land" is not our true habitat, and these good neighbors are not the pilgrim people to whom we belong. So we sure sinners dream on, dreaming of the divine domain come on Earth as it is in heaven. We dream of the new order already begun amid the old.

The brothers said, "Here comes the dreamer." We are Joseph, and this we know: We have been here before with the ancestors, through other reformations and transformations. We dreamed different dreams then, but they, too, were dreams of faith.

This time we dream of Ecumenical and Ecological Earth. And we dream of the baptized life as Earth-honoring faith. "The baptized life" . . . so of course we must talk of water, the waters of life of baptism and the waters of life of the planet.

What is the substance of baptism? How do the waters of life both capture and forge the way of discipleship? To borrow from baptismal liturgies, is being water-washed and Spirit-borne, and "remembering our baptism" with wet branches waved over the congregation, a quiet formation of moral orientation and courage? Consider this. Paul has to explain his innovative missionary policy of bringing Jews and Gentiles together in community in terms that honor the outsiders as insiders. In 2 Corinthians 5:17 he does so, saying: "When anyone is united to Christ, there is a new world; the old order has gone, and a new order has already begun."

Baptism is the focal practice that celebrates this new world, in which previous ethnic identities and inherited social definitions are both transcended and eliminated in Christ. Paul, speaking to the Galatians, could hardly be more explicit about baptism initiating a new people by crossing and canceling the boundaries that the world insists upon: "Baptized in Christ, you are clothed in Christ, and there is neither Jew nor Greek, slave nor free, neither male nor female; you are all one in Christ Jesus" (Galatians 3:28).

This baptism of both Jews and Gentiles in one community is itself an improvisation on a Jewish practice, and it initiates what Paul deems a "new creation." It is one in which enmity as the dividing wall between peoples is broken down and peace is made, now in the form of a new multiethnic community named "a new humanity" in Christ (Ephesians 2:14, 15). And don't overlook that this new human reality is the church's message to "the principalities and powers" concerning the way of God (Ephesians 3:10). In different words, baptism both celebrates and effects the concrete community alternative to empire and empire's rule by division. Empires use differences (Jew/Gentile, male/female, slave/free) to separate people, set them against one another, and rule them. In baptism the new status is a new kind of social relationship that overarches the differences in a new unity.

I add only what we all know: how baptism and discipleship went wildly wrong when Christianity itself decided to ally its fate and its faith with empire. Then faith ends up mimicking empire, and baptism is stood on its head—becoming the means to *exclusive* membership in the only true imperial faith, Christianity, rather than the new order begun in the midst of the old. What was to be a Torah community of Jews and Gentiles became instead, with Constantine's sword and Charlemagne's offer that few could refuse ("Be baptized or die!"), murderous to the Jews and numerous other communities of outsiders over the centuries. So perhaps we cannot any longer even sense the profound moral substance of baptism as a reconciling, community-creating, interethnic unity on egalitarian and nonviolent terms.

Is "the water of life" no more than a metaphor, then? What about the literal waters of life so many are deprived of? Are there neglected dimensions of baptism we had best attend to now, for our tipping-point time?

There is a scene in Marilynne Robinson's novel *Gilead* where the old pastor writes this: "You and Tobias are hopping around in the sprinkler. The sprinkler is a magnificent invention because it exposes raindrops to sunshine. That does occur in nature, but it is rare. When I was in seminary I used to go sometimes to the Baptists down at the river. It was something to see the preacher lifting the one who was being baptized up out of the water and the water pouring off the garments and the hair. It did look like a birth or a resurrection. For us the water just heightens the touch of the pastor's hand on the sweet bones of the head, sort of like making an electrical connection. I've always loved to baptize people, though I have sometimes wished there were more shimmer and splash involved in the way we go about it. Well, but you two are dancing around in your iridescent little downpour, whooping and stomping as sane people ought to do when they encounter a thing so miraculous as water."

The waters of life. Sane people should do some good whooping and stomping, with a little shimmer and splash, when they encounter a thing so miraculous as water! You were born in it, in your mother's warm womb waters, and it's surer than taxes that without it you die. Millions have lived without love; no critter in all creation has lived without water. Life itself likely emerged from the waters of the sea, and most life is still in the salty brine. Water births, it cleanses and purifies, it heals, it revives, it transports, it rains down and wells up. The planet, in fact, should be dubbed "Water," not "Earth," since it's 70 percent H_2O. And all the rest—that other 30 percent—depends utterly on this miniscule molecule sent from heaven above.

The waters of life. When will you know that God has been raptured to Earth and the New Jerusalem has descended from heaven? Not when houses of worship are planted on every corner. There is no temple in that redeemed city, as there was no temple in Eden, and no empire. There is the throne of God *and* "the river of the water of life, bright as crystal, flowing from the throne of God and of the Lamb through the middle of the street of the city. On either side of the river is the tree of life, with its twelve kinds of fruit, producing its fruit each month; and the leaves of the tree are for the healing of the nations" (Revelations 22:1–2, echoing Ezekiel).

"Flowing from the throne of God and of the Lamb"— the *baptized* Lamb, baptized in the river Jordan by John the Baptizer. And did you know that just as you breathe the same air Jesus did, so too you were baptized in the same water as Jesus the Lamb, just a different river or a different Samaritan well? The sum of water has been fixed since prehistoric times, far longer than we late-arrivers have been spilling it, splashing in it, and baptizing with it. So be forewarned: Jehovah's not making any more of the waters of life.

I am not by nature an alarmist—Lutherans don't get alarmed, they just go quiet and take to prayer and choral music and beer. But I live in the droughted Southwest. No one is towing melting ice caps to Santa Fe, and I can sense Edna Jacques's lament from the Dirty Thirties (she was a Saskatchewan farmer's wife and a noted Canadian poet):

> The crop has failed again, the wind and sun
> Dried out the stubble first, then one by one
> The strips of summerfallow, seared with heat,
> Crunched, like old fallen leaves, our lovely wheat,
> The garden is a dreary blighted waste,
> The very air is gritty to the taste.

Yet we, the thirsty, gather in worship in Santa Fe. Here is a call to worship in our congregation:

> We gather to worship God, the Lord, and Giver of Life
>> *God gives us the waters of life.*
>
> In the deserts of our lives, in the wilderness within,
>> *God gives us the waters of life.*
>
> To give us hope when our lives run dry, to give us strength when our world seems barren,
>> *God gives us the waters of life.*
>
> To let peace flow like a river and love spring forth life a fountain,
>> *God gives us the waters of life.*
>
> To make justice roll down like waters and righteousness like an everlasting stream,
>> *God gives us the waters of life.*

And here is what greets us in the sanctuary:

The nave on one side is a wall of glass, adobe mud brick, and timbers. It is the eye's passageway into the high mountain desert of which the sanctuary is a part: piñon and juniper scatter themselves across sandy loam like the sower's seed on arid ground; chamisa and cottonwoods await the next rush of rain in the arroyo; the Sangre de Cristo Mountains rise close in; and the desert sun floods yellow into the sanctuary. The sun rays glisten at the base of the glass, dancing on the moving water that runs the full length of the eastern wall. That long trough is the baptismal font, if "font" isn't too feeble a word for an acequia, the desert irrigation ditch used for a thousand years in this valley by Pueblo Indian peoples and four hundred years by Hispanic farmers.

Acequias bear waters of life to this day. The desert blooms along them like an Isaiah vision. Without them, we do not eat or laugh.

The waters of life of the font, and the acequia waters flowing in the desert: something sacred, something essential from womb to tomb, is borne by the waters precisely *as* water, and our bodies know it in every watery cell. It is the Creator's presence, incarnate and full of life.

So, friends, will your ministries and your practices become that second tipping point—creating, with the grace of God, a way of life that is set, like a bulwark never failing, against the slow tsunami of planetary degradation? Will our spirits and deeds join the ecological reformation for a different Earth-human community? Will we Joseph dreamers be Joseph the *wise* dreamer, who, yes, right in the midst of Pharaoh's court, conserves and preserves Earth's bounty in the fat years so as to sustain Earth's life in the lean years?

For this is where our lives are now, trembling in the balance between two tipping points in what will be the century of the environment, the century of religion, and the century of the economy. One tipping point is physical and social change of, well, biblical proportions. It is geophysical change bearing a strong human imprint, and it is under way. The other tipping point is our long-delayed conversion to Earth-honoring faith *for* the century of the environment, of the economy, and of religion.

I close with words lifted from a sermon by a pastor friend in Virginia, Janet Parker. Let the clean water of baptism "wash away any indifference you have, any despair you feel, any fear which clouds your vision. And let it symbolize the outpouring of the Holy Spirit upon a transformed people. Let it remind us of the thirst of the earth and the thirst of the people in many parts of the world who live parched lives. Let it remind us of the dream of children to dance and bathe and drink clean water. Let it remind us of the promise of scripture that streams will break forth in the desert, and that the river of the water of death will be replaced by the river of the water of life."

So there it is: the throne of God in the midst of the city, with the rivers of the waters of life flowing from it. How can we, the baptized, *keep* from singing?

Larry Rasmussen is Reinhold Niebuhr Professor Emeritus, Union Theological Seminary, New York City, and author of the award-winning volume Earth Community, Earth Ethics *(Orbis Books). He lives in Santa Fe, New Mexico. This essay is adapted from a sermon delivered in August 2007 at the Ghost Ranch Peace Week Worship in Abiquiu, New Mexico, which in turn was based on a commencement address given at the Lutheran Theological Seminary at Chicago in May 2007.*

Holy Land

Janisse Ray

I am kneeling with my family in our upstairs study, a child in the house of my childhood. My knees are on a pillow, my forehead against the back of a chair, and I am praying out loud, calling one word—the name of Jesus—over and over. Six of us, my mother and father and brothers and sister, are in the room, and we are all calling. Outside, dusk has drawn its curtains around our home; inside, lights are extinguished, and my family is kneeling in the dark surrounded by books, calling on Jesus. My voice is muffled by my arms and my waist-length hair, which shutters my face. I know God hears us. I think he is going to show up. I don't know what will happen when he does.

"We're going to have tarrying service tonight," my father had said at dinner, which is lunch in the South. We looked at him, careful to hide our feelings, then glanced at each other, faces blank. "After supper," he said. Sometimes we had tarrying services at church, but mostly church was too far away to go—over an hour each way—and since God had not yet appeared in our midst, touching us and causing us to get up and dance and speak in tongues, we had to tarry extra.

My father would say to you: "I raised her to love and fear God." His quest for spiritual truth and communion with God was the overarching and consistent theme of my childhood. In that search my father abandoned the ways of the world and turned to the ways of God. That search led him to the Bible, led him on Sunday mornings to the doorway of the Church of the Lord Jesus Christ of the Apostolic Faith in Brunswick, Georgia, and led him to require us to sit beside the radio as he tuned in "the broadcast," which is what he called the sermons of Bishop Johnson and, later, Bishop Shelton, whom he believed to be the thirteenth and fourteenth apostles of Christ.

I was expected, in every moment, waking and not, to seek the Holy Spirit, and in many ways I have not let my father down. Of course we were not to swear or steal or kill—those were unthinkable sins. We were also not to wear jewelry or compete or wear makeup or pants (we girls) or celebrate pagan holidays like Christmas and Easter. Smoking cigarettes vilified the temple that was our body. After the blessing at every meal, each person at the table was required to recite a Bible verse.

Later my father would say to me, quietly and in the trusting manner of a man who would not open carelessly the deepest recesses of his soul, that he believed the spirit of a human was a huge thing. We were standing beside a highway once when my father told me this. I was driving back to my home, hours away. My parents were standing beside my car, beside the highway, saying goodbye. As my father spoke, he drew his hands wide, circumscribing the air that turned to clouds, the shade from endless trees, the ground that went for miles below our feet. "Most people think that the spirit is a tiny thing in the human body," he said. "But I believe that the body is a small manifestation of the spirit."

Two thin threads attach any human to a religion, and those are tradition and belief. As for tradition, to follow the ways of family, of history, and of culture, and thus fall into a particular religion, is easy. But one also needs faith. To worship an unprovable deity is to "have faith." Faith is "the substance of things hoped for and the evidence of things not seen" (Hebrews I:II).

I lost my faith. As I matured into adulthood, my thinking grew more and more empirical, and a belief in eternal life and a creator became harder for me, until it became downright impossible.

As I began to venture into nature—up mountains and down rivers and into ravines—I began to encounter the feeling I had had as a young girl when I knew Jesus was listening.

But because I come from people who believe in spirit, and who believe in ghosts (or at least one Holy Ghost), and because these ideas were demonstrated to me often and from a very young age, I have had to contend with spirit as an idea and a reality, despite biology professors and other intellectuals who are unafraid to believe wholeheartedly in the human body as animal, as creature, as biomass that will die and rot and become nutrients for more life.

It has been my great fortune to tread in the wilderness, simply looking at rocks and trees and waters, and suddenly find a thing I did not come looking for. How many times have I encountered this unassailable feeling, a knowledge, that I was in the presence of something holy, divine, and transcendent in which I could find faith and in which revelations would be given to me. Lo and behold, God was in the old growth longleaf pine and in the cypress swamp and in the desert and on the mountaintop and in the coral reefs and in frozen rivers. In those places I could not help but worship, without prayer, without tithing, without fasting, without tarrying. Being there was worship.

Once I saw a small wooden building alongside a highway through the Ocala National Forest in central Florida. A sign on the roadside chapel, which had no parsonage or parking lot, said Forest Community Church. I thought then, with some elation, *This is the church for me.* "Revelation comes in two volumes," said Thomas Aquinas, "the Bible and nature." The volume I could read has been nature.

I have been known to say that I am not a person of faith, but that is not true. Although I personally have no faith in a human-like god, or in many gods, or in the promise of heaven or the threat of hell, or indeed in any afterlife at all, I have faith.

It is early morning and I am snorkeling in Florida's Crystal River. Although the water is 72 degrees, the November air is chilly, and to keep warm I stay submerged. I am wearing a mask, floating at the edge of Three Sisters Springs. I am here to see manatees. In the light green water, I can't see more than ten or twelve feet, so at first I am frightened when two monstrous shapes materialize out of the gloom. They are so big. They glide past, so close that I reach out and touch one. The manatee turns, positioning itself alongside me, then rolls over and presents its belly. Its hide is rough and thick, covered with barnacles and algae. Its fins are like arms, its tail huge and rounded. Slowly it paddles on. Three others come. Go. Five appear.

Now, below, I can make out manatees lying on the river bottom, in deep silt, sometimes atop each other, a fat knot of sea cows. The scene is surreal. I start to become manatee. I wave my feet and glide. What interests me this morning is a cathedral of water, and how the rays of new sun refract to points in front of me in this water kingdom. I glide and roll. I quit using my hands, and when a manatee approaches, I put my goggled head against his side.

A mother and calf dispatch from the group. The calf, curious, quits nursing when he sees me. He swims and tumbles and looks me in the eyes, and I roll with him, breathing when

I reach the surface. The mother rubs her body against mine and rolls. She does this again and again. With her searching eyes she examines me. She puts her face next to mine, looking deep.

Within all the unknown, the manatee and I enter another plane, which is wordless and weightless, fluid, a beautiful lightness that has to be spirit. Her eye is a wrinkled spiral, beseeching. Her spirit is big and it has merged with my spirit, which is likewise big. Something rises in me that has been rising for a long time.

I have faith in the Earth and the things of the Earth. I have faith that they will nourish and keep me, all the days of my life.

Janisse Ray grew up in a junkyard along U.S. Highway 1. She is the author of Wild Card Quilt *and* Ecology of a Cracker Childhood, *which won the American Book Award, as well as the Southern Book Critics Circle Award, Southeastern Booksellers Association Award for Nonfiction, and the Southern Environmental Law Center Award. A naturalist, environmental activist, and winner of the 1996 Merriam Frontier Award, she has also published her work in* Wild Earth, Orion, Florida Naturalist, *and* Georgia Wildlife *and has been a nature commentator for Georgia Public Radio. She lives in Vermont and Georgia.*

The Ripple Effect

Tri Robinson

When I was a boy in the 1950s, my family traditionally visited the national parks of the western United States. Summer after summer, we would venture to places like Zion, Bryce, Yellowstone, and Yosemite National Parks, tent-camping from the back of our wood-sided Oldsmobile station wagon. My parents wanted us to experience and develop an appreciation for the magnificent natural beauty of those preserved places.

With each vacation adventure, my appreciation deepened. The things I saw were etched in my memory and helped mold me into someone who will forever value God's creation. The grandeur, the color, the immensity of canyons and rock that had been formed by the sure powers of nature filled my young mind with awe. What I experienced was truly beautiful in every way, and it spoke to me, even at my young age, of something greater than itself. I was struck with the realization that all of it had been designed and sculpted with imagination and for a purpose.

Our family loved to explore the nooks and crannies of the places we visited. It was on one such exploration that I experienced the most beautiful lake I had ever seen. Crystal Lake (as I'll call it) was truly everything the park ranger had promised the evening before in his fireside nature talk and slide presentation. Following his instructions, we headed for the trail to the lake, climbing the steep rocky path for a mile and a half, past showering falls, before cresting a rocky, jagged ridge. We then descended into a pocket of granite that held a large pool of water so absolutely clear, so serene and so pure, that it took our breath away. To this day I can remember looking into the depths of that pool and thinking it must be bottomless.

Twenty years later, in the mid-1970s, I revisited that park in hopes of reliving those fond memories. I was now married, with a two-year-old daughter who loved to view everything from a baby carrier on my back. The colors and the canyons were as beautiful as I remembered, but the campgrounds had become congested and somewhat more sophisticated. The campfire singing and other quiet sounds that had once filled the evening air were replaced by the purr of generators that powered self-contained campers and motor homes.

Time has a way of changing things; though disappointing, this is not surprising. What struck me the most on this trip, however, were the subtle yet profound changes in and around

Crystal Lake. The path I remembered so well was now paved, and the fragile undergrowth that once had grown up to the lake's rocky shoreline had receded due to increased foot traffic. The impaired clarity of the water reminded me of a cataract on an eye that once had perfect vision. Despite the posted signs (which in themselves detracted from the innocence and purity of the setting), there were bits of toilet paper and litter in the undergrowth, and a soda can was visible in the pool itself. Something precious had been lost: not merely a young man's memory but something far greater, something I felt was precious to the Creator himself. It struck me then that this was more than an issue of ecological concern: it was an issue of morality.

The Crystal Lake scenario is a familiar heartbreak to anyone who loves and spends time in the untouched places of nature. Humankind's disruption of the purity of creation goes deeper than science and politics; it offends more than the human intellect because it touches the inner consciousness of the heart. It feels inherently wrong and, in a very true sense, immoral. The apostle Paul once wrote, "From the time the world was created, people have seen the earth and sky and all that God made. They can clearly see his invisible qualities—his eternal power and divine nature. So they have no excuse whatsoever for not knowing God" (Romans 1:20).

We call creation "nature" because it exposes us to the very nature of God. Seeing the miracle of its purity, its creativity, and its perfect order gives humankind a glimpse of who God is. This makes the existence of unblemished nature a deeply spiritual matter. If there is to be any hope of preserving creation for future generations from the molestation of human endeavor, this must be recognized as the spiritual and moral issue it most certainly is.

When a stone is thrown into the heart of a still pool of water, ripples move outward from the point of impact until they reach the grasses and reeds of the shoreline. So it will be with this important issue of creation's care. Environmental stewardship must begin in the hearts of people. If the heart is polluted with unresolved sin, with selfishness and greed, this pollution will ripple to the mind, which in turn will affect the actions and behavior of the body. If the heart is pure, the mind will be renewed and transformed (Romans 12:1–4). And if our minds are renewed, we will no longer be so self-focused and self-absorbed. As we grasp the mind of Christ, we will become other-centered, concerned about the world around us and about the generations to come.

The declining condition of the environment is a moral and heart issue and must be addressed accordingly. When people have changed their mind-sets, then their attitudes, behaviors, and actions will change too, becoming responsible and right. They will adjust their lifestyles to sacrifice for things that are worthy of sacrifice. These actions will first affect the family, then neighbors, the community, and ultimately the world. Through such changes of heart and mind, the potential for improving global environmental conditions can be fulfilled. When people make choices beyond their own interests—supporting causes that contribute to social justice rather than personal gain—our world and its environment will improve considerably.

Deteriorating environmental conditions around the world are the cause of much human suffering. Children in developing nations are dying because of pollution and the lack of uncontaminated water. Famine is on the rise from the loss of fertile soil due to urbanization and the erosion of clear-cut lands. It is time to take action. When hearts are changed, people begin to care and to take radical steps. Hope for the environment begins with hearts that have undergone an environmental cleanup, and this is only available through the gracious miraculous work of the Creator himself.

Tri Robinson is senior pastor of Vineyard Christian Fellowship of Boise. He is also the founder of Let's Tend the Garden, an environmental stewardship ministry that serves as a model for churches across the country, and that was featured in Is God Green? *a 2006 PBS special with Bill Moyers.*

With a degree in education and biology (his master's thesis was on the ecology of the Pacific Northwest), Robinson became a secondary-school science teacher for twelve years before entering full-time ministry in 1982. On mission trips among remote hill tribes on the border of Thailand and Burma, he and his family observed the devastating impact of an overused, damaged environment on people who depended on the land. *After years of Bible study and teaching, Robinson came to the realization that environmental stewardship is not only an overlooked truth of the Christian faith but also a value largely neglected by the church.*

Along with fulfilling his responsibilities at Vineyard Boise, Robinson is in demand as a speaker at conferences, where he helps transfer his working insights and experience to a wide spectrum of church leaders. He is the author of three books, Saving God's Green Earth, Revolutionary Leadership, *and* Small Footprint, Large Handprint.

The Shalom Principle

Peter Sawtell

For more than thirty years, I have been on a personal faith-journey into an ever-deepening environmental perspective. Throughout these decades, a rich variety of experiences has shaped my knowledge, my values, my commitments, and ultimately my vocation. The winding path has involved profound experiences in the outdoors, extensive undergraduate studies in ecology, and several waves of environmental activism. The religious part of my journey includes five years of pastoring in a farming community, participating in the emerging ecumenical environmental movement, and substantial changes in my theology and ethics. For example, the witness of faith-based activists opened my eyes to the realities of environmental racism, both in painful particularities of local communities and in broad statistical patterns.

Then, in the mid-1990s, I experienced a genuinely life-changing moment when the catastrophic scope of global climate change moved from my head into my heart. In preparation for a church presentation, I spent a week investigating the emerging research on global warming. As I read about unprecedented transformations to our planet's ecology, my growing intellectual understanding was joined by profound grief, fear, compassion, and anger. Science, theology, and personal emotions converged, driving home the urgency of this crisis in a way that permanently changed my worldview.

The interconnection between my Christian faith and my concern about the state of the Earth led me, in the summer of 2000, to establish Eco-Justice Ministries, an agency that does environmental work with churches. I believe that the theological notion of eco-justice—the well-being of all humanity on a thriving Earth—is an important principle for engaging churches in environmental action.

But although I have spent thirty years acquiring knowledge and formulating my beliefs, I often get barely thirty minutes to bring some of my insights to the church groups I work with. In that half hour, I have the challenge of guiding a group of strangers into an awareness of the depth and complexity of our world's ecological crisis and helping them discern why religious institutions are so important in addressing that crisis. In that very short time, I can't begin to convey the richness of my passion—yet it is enough time to draw people into the perspective that is at the core of my work.

With a large sheet of newsprint and some markers as my tools, I invite members of a discussion group to list the environmental issues they care about and hear about in the news. It does not take them long to create an extensive list. All the people in every church group I've met with know something about a lot of issues, and they are deeply concerned.

They name clean air and clean water, global warming, and rain forests. They list toxic wastes, coral reefs, and the hole in the ozone. Urban sprawl, water shortages, soil erosion, spreading deserts, species extinction, overfished oceans, invasive species, the dead zone in the Gulf of Mexico, mercury in fish, and lead paint in older housing are among the issues that go on the worksheet. Global issues share space with close-to-home concerns about a special place, a locally unique species, or a controversial community issue.

As the brainstorming goes on, we add details to some lines. A general concern about water expands to cover different causes of water pollution, the impact of dams and wells, worldwide shortages of freshwater, soil damaged by overirrigation, and the new cultural foolishness of bottled water. Often the list starts to look like a web, as relationships between scattered topics become evident. Asthma-causing air pollution, toxic waste dumps, lead paint, and transportation issues are all linked to urban poverty. One person's comment about agriculture might encourage others to talk about the overuse of fertilizer, the health impacts of pesticides on farmworkers, sewage from factory farming, water for irrigation, farmland used for biofuels, and greenhouse gases emitted by belching cattle.

When the sheet of newsprint is filled, I call a stop, and we spend a few moments staring at the list, letting it all soak in. There's a stunned, painful silence as ordinary church people realize how much they know about the Earth's deep distress.

I reassure them that I didn't ask them to create the list to make them depressed. ("Too late!" someone usually shouts.) We created that long list of complex, interconnected issues, I say, so that we could become aware of a very basic lesson. When so many things are going wrong—when the problems are so big, so important, and so intertwined—we need a shift in our perspective. Rather than considering an overwhelming list of many discrete issues, I ask the people to take a larger view. With that shift to a broader perspective, we can see a different kind of problem, and a different kind of solution.

All the issues on the newsprint are just symptoms of one central, essential problem: humans are living out of whack with the Earth. In our modern industrial world, we are living in a distorted, dysfunctional relationship with the rest of creation. "We don't have environmental problems," I say. "We have a human problem."

Embedded in the governing mind-set of our culture are fundamental flaws in how we understand our connections with the natural world. We have seen humanity as separate from the rest of creation. We have looked at the world as a storehouse of resources, rather than as a dynamic and interdependent system. We have been oblivious to the world's limits, both in what it can provide and in the abuse that it can absorb. We have arrogantly claimed the wisdom and power to manipulate the world, without an adequate understanding of the consequences. We have been selfishly fixated on our immediate wants and needs without considering future generations. These sorts of misunderstandings are the basis for the issues listed on the sheet of newsprint.

Yes, there is much work to be done on technical matters like energy efficiency and pollution control. We do need to craft public policy and economic incentives. But if changes in policy and technology are to take us in genuinely new directions, we will have to change our beliefs, our assumptions, and our expectations. We need to claim a new way of living in relationship with the entire Earth community.

If we look for solutions primarily through technical fixes, then churches are going to be fringe players. If we seek the core solutions through detailed changes in public policy, it will be very hard to mobilize the politically diverse constituencies of congregations for advocacy and action.

But when we see the environmental crisis as a human problem, religious communities suddenly become very important. If we're struggling with a warped notion of humanity's place and purpose in creation, then faith communities have vast expertise in dealing with that problem.

In religious communities we know how to deal with the question of what it means to be human, and thus are superbly positioned to address the human problem at the heart of our current crisis. At the core of our mission, we focus on the meaning of life and on what really constitutes the good life. For centuries, we have been addressing relationships and community—not always getting the answers right, of course, but always circling around these themes. We deal with matters of justice and ethics. Perhaps most important, we claim to bring transformation to individuals, communities, and society, precisely by inviting people to adopt new understandings of our relationship with God, with the whole human family, and with the creation.

To bring about such transformation, we must tell new stories about who we are and where we are going. We need a sense of our neighbors that reaches around the world to include people from all countries, people far in the future, and our fellow creatures of other species. We must see ourselves as cooperative, not controlling, in our relationship with nature. The challenge of making these shifts in perspective are not exclusively religious, but they are challenges that must be taken on by any faith that claims to address the needs of today's world.

Many people in the Judeo-Christian tradition look to the opening stories in the book of Genesis for instruction about humanity's relation to the rest of creation. In the story of Eden, the Earthling is told to "till and keep" the garden—or in a more literal translation, to "serve" the soil of the garden. In the poetic account of the seven days of creation, humans are assigned a more complex—and, for many today, more controversial—role of dominion in maintaining the Earth's fragile order. These creation stories have a tremendous mythic power in our culture and have been, perhaps, involved in our abuse of the Earth as we have muddled their two distinctive messages and confused dominion with domination. Historically and theologically, we need to pay attention to these Genesis narratives, but the call to care for creation is not found only in those few chapters.

My sense of what constitutes a faithful relationship with God's creation is rooted in a much larger scriptural theme. I find great wisdom and hope in the biblical principle of shalom—of peace with justice. The Jewish and Christian faith traditions, through thousands of years, have affirmed that God wills shalom for all of creation. The goodness of this delicately balanced Earth is diminished when we abuse or exploit any part of it. We are bound to all other parts of creation in complex, fragile relationships, and shalom guides us toward justice, compassion, and solidarity in all of them.

The biblical vision of shalom provides a rich ethical grounding for addressing our current needs. It guides us toward sufficiency—"enough"—instead of overconsumption.

It demands that we seek sustainability. It reassures us that we can find justice and peace as we move into appropriate relationships with all of our neighbors. The promising hope of shalom gives us the good news that a different and ecologically responsible way of living is one not of sacrifice and denial but of joy and fulfillment.

I see the next thirty years as a time of unprecedented challenge for all of humanity. The threats of global climate change, water shortages, collapsing fisheries, and many other symptoms bring a great sense of urgency. Within just a few decades, the human family must make profound changes in our collective ecological footprint. We must do so in a way that embodies special concern for the poorest, and that demands special accountability from the wealthy and powerful.

If we are to avert disaster, we humans must adopt a self-understanding very different from the one that led us into this crisis. Our rapid movement toward new social structures, new technologies, new laws, and new economic principles must be guided by a transformed awareness. We will grow into a new sense of ourselves as being enmeshed with creation as we make mindful choices in the marketplace, the voting booth, and our neighborhoods.

It is my hope and my daily prayer that the world's churches and other religious institutions will awake to this challenge. I pray that, in denominations and congregations, committed and faithful people will provide enlightened leadership that can guide us all toward a joyous, just, and sustainable way of living within God's creation.

The Reverend Peter Sawtell (ministry@eco-justice.org) *is an ordained minister in the United Church of Christ and serves as executive director of Eco-Justice Ministries. Based in Denver, Colorado, this ecumenical agency provides church leaders across the country with resources for worship and education, perspectives on environmental theology and spirituality, strategies for social change, practical steps for environmental living, opportunities to collaborate with environmental and justice organizations, and encouragement for political action. And, as a member of the Religious Environmental Leaders Group, Sawtell works in close collaboration with the major faith-based environmental groups in the United States.*

The Zaytuna Ruku Tree

Zaid Shakir

A tree that looks at God all day,
And lifts her leafy arms to pray . . .
　　　—*Joyce Kilmer*, "Trees"

In this great American poem, Joyce Kilmer captures the beauty, majesty, and awe found in one of God's most intriguing creatures, the tree. One thing that intrigued Kilmer, and possibly all others who would take time to reflect on this marvelous creation, is the tree's constant and intimate communion with God.

Before such a powerfully reverent creation, Kilmer can only sense his own inadequacy and weakness. We humans can produce wonderful, eloquent poetry, but what is a poem, which emerges from our frail pens, compared to the timeless wisdom embodied in a tree—a simple yet infinitely complex creation wrought by the marvelous hand of God?

Zaytuna is an educational institute and school for the study of Islam in a manner that brings light into the world. In 1998, the institute moved to its current home in Hayward, California, inheriting a rugged lot with piles of trash and an aging pine tree that appeared to be nearing its demise. However, not long after prayer and the study of sacred knowledge began on the property, this tree revived, its branches flourishing with new growth. Over time, as it stretched itself outward, offering more and more shade, its leaning posture became unmistakably akin to the *ruku* position of Muslim prayer. It became known as the "Ruku Tree."

Many of us here at the Zaytuna Institute were awed by the Ruku Tree, seemingly bowed by the travails of time into a reverent prayer position. This graceful bowing made her shade, her invigorating aroma, and, for a legion of youthful climbers, her tempting branches all the more accessible. Some of the greatest contemporary scholars of Islam sat in her shade. Sacred knowledge was conveyed under her vigilant watch. And from the refuge she represented, many students and teachers paused to watch as the winter rain gently caressed the green grass spread out before her.

The reverent, bowing tree had not yet completed her life's work, however. She had a final call to answer. God says in the Qur'an, "The stars and the trees prostrate [unto Him]" (Al-Qur'an 55:6). Observers of the Zaytuna Ruku Tree over the years noticed that she was inching ever closer to her own prostration. Therefore, it came as no surprise when, on a fateful, rainy winter night, she completed her devotion, prostrating totally to her Lord. Her majestic head nestled firmly upon the ground, her massive trunk oriented itself toward the prayer direction, her toes, partially uprooted, curved beneath her. Her life's work done, she is now gone.

The wood from the Ruku Tree was carefully harvested and used in the creative arts. A new tree will be planted soon in her place, Insha'Allah.

Like the tree Kilmer praised, which highlighted his mortality and whose majesty served to alert him to the reality of an all-powerful God, our tree served a similar purpose for many in our community. Kilmer died shortly after penning his poem, gunned down in the killing fields of France during the insanity of the First World War, having barely passed his twenty-second birthday. I am sure that the passing of our tree reminds many of us at Zaytuna of our own mortality. There is no permanence in this lower abode. Perhaps it is not coincidental that the very chapter that mentions the prostration of the trees also reminds us: "All that is on the earth will perish" (Al-Qur'an 55:26). Reminders of this fact surround us. Who among us will take heed?

"Have you not seen how God sets forth a parable? A good word is like a good tree whose roots are firm and whose branches reach heaven. It gives its fruit during every season, by leave of its Lord. And God sets forth parables to people that they may remember" (Al-Qur'an 14: 24–25).

Imam Zaid Shakir was born in Berkeley, California, and accepted Islam in 1977 while serving in the U.S. Air Force. He earned a bachelor of arts degree in international relations at American University in Washington, D.C., and a master's degree in political science from Rutgers University. While overseas in Egypt, Syria, and Morocco, he studied Arabic and traditional Islamic sciences, including Islamic law, the Qur'an, and Islamic spirituality. Settling in New Haven, Connecticut, he cofounded Masjid Al-Islam and the Tri-State Muslim Education Initiative, and taught political science at South-ern Connecticut State University. He has written numerous articles for peri-odicals; translated several books from Arabic into English, including Heirs of the Prophets; *and authored a volume of essays,* Scattered Pictures: Reflections of an American Muslim *(2005).*

Imam Shakir is currently a scholar-in-residence at the Zaytuna Institute in Hayward, California, where he teaches courses in Arabic, Islamic law, history, and Islamic spirituality. A frequent speaker at local and national Muslim events, he has emerged as one of the nation's leading Islamic scholars and a voice of conscience for American Muslims and non-Muslims alike.

Colored Town and Liberation Science

Kristin Shrader-Frechette

My favorite Sundays of my Kentucky childhood were those when we traveled to Colored Town (as everyone then called it), on the outskirts of Danville. Dad woke us for early Mass and, still in our church clothes, we began the three-hour drive to see "Grandma," Catherine Jackman. Dad was always at the wheel of our old black Hudson, and Mom was often turning and talking over the front seat, telling stories about her childhood in Colored Town. When we turned onto its unpaved main street, our car never moved more than a few yards before people gathered and stopped it in the middle of the dirt road. Shouting "It's Millie and the kids!" they always pulled open the doors and began hugging everyone. As Mom darted out of the car, straight for Catherine's house, she always hugged people along the way.

Colored Town's main street was usually empty. Few could afford cars, and most people walked several miles to their jobs.

None of the homes was painted, and all of them had outhouses and pumps out back, even in the late 1950s. Yet across the front, most homes had big covered wooden porches with rocking chairs and swings—porches where people sat and visited, told stories, and drank iced tea.

More than eighty years ago, Catherine Jackman became one of the first African-American women to graduate from Centre College in Danville. She had hoped for a career in teaching, but despite her superb grades and the state's chronic shortage of teachers, no Kentucky school would hire her. After months of searching for employment, Catherine took the only job she was offered, that of seamstress at Danville's Rainbow Cleaners. My grandfather owned the Rainbow. Inside the cleaners, Grandpa said, customers always would speak politely to Catherine. He was outraged that, outside the shop, she became invisible to the same people. No whites spoke to her as she passed them on the street.

On a steamy Kentucky evening in the 1920s, Grandpa's young wife was stricken with mosquito-borne encephalitis. It left her an invalid, and she was sent to Kentucky State Hospital, the only place able to care for her. Alone with a three-year-old daughter, Mildred, Grandpa lapsed into despair, then alcoholism. Catherine managed the shop every day, but his alcoholism only worsened. Soon Catherine was bringing little Millie home with her each evening to Colored Town. There Mom lived until she married Dad at eighteen. From Catherine, Millie found her deep laugh, her beautiful singing voice, her quick wit, her unmatched cooking and sewing skills, and her habit of hugging people as soon as she saw them.

Mildred House Shrader became a leader in Kentucky civil-rights causes and was active in both the women's movement and the peace movement. She was the first white member of the Kentucky NAACP. When Mom and Dad marched and sang in civil-rights protests, they often brought some of us seven children with them, pulling the two youngest in our rusting, red "Radio Flyer" wagon.

Mom and Dad designed and built our home in the only racially integrated part of Jefferson County—in Fern Creek, near the large African-American community of Newburg. Our large front porch stretched across the entire house, and it had rocking chairs and a wooden swing, just like the homes in Colored Town. By the early 1960s it was common for newborn girls in Newburg to be christened "Mildred," for their white godmother. Some of my sisters and brothers also made their best friends in Newburg. My younger brother Christopher and his friend Walter ("Bubba," they called each other) spent a good deal of time thinking up ways to get the better of the local racists. Once Chris bought a family membership in the local Moose Club, then mentioned that he and his "brother" would stop by to play pool. When they did so, Walter would be the only colored face in a room full of whites, mostly pickup-truck owners. The ensuing situations, with Chris and

Walter repeating their deadpan exchanges, made for raucous dinnertime stories. Chris and Walter would always "win" such conflicts, at least in the retelling.

Devout Catholics, Mom and Dad believed that the test of genuine religion was whether believers served the poor and the powerless. Mom liked the idea of Dante, that the hottest places in hell are reserved for those who remain neutral in times of great moral crisis. Some of her heroes were Catholic peace activist Daniel Berrigan, United Farm Workers' founder Cesar Chavez, *Catholic Worker* founder Dorothy Day, union leader Mother Jones, and Trappist monk Thomas Merton. When her seventh child went to school, Mom finally was able to go to college. There she discovered a name for what she and Dad had been living, and what martyred San Salvador Archbishop Oscar Romero and others like him preached: "liberation theology." Condemning poverty, injustice, and colonialism, liberation theologians argue that following the Gospel requires not only belief but also working for justice, exercising what Latin American bishops and later popes have called a "preferential option for the poor."

Mom was the first activist that we knew. She had no tolerance for injustice, hypocrisy, or false piety—and she said so. She thought Chavez and Day were right. Talk is cheap; people show what they believe by how they live. As children, we often were embarrassed by Mom's outspokenness and fearlessness. Sometimes we wished that she would just stay home, keep quiet, and get on with canning garden vegetables and caring for us. When our friends came to visit, we pleaded with her not to say anything controversial. Not until I was sixteen did I fully realize how fortunate we all were to have her. Not until she was dying, in 1970, did I realize how profoundly she had shaped all of us.

After college, Mom began the career that Catherine never had. When she was diagnosed with bone cancer, she had been teaching high-school English for only a year in the poorest slum in Louisville. Mom had the first environmentally induced cancer that I had encountered, caused by unnecessary and repeated x-rays. Years later, the U.S. Office of Technology Assessment confirmed that up to 90 percent of all cancers are "environmentally induced and theoretically preventable." Mom need not have died at forty-five. Her death put a human face on society's monumental failure to adequately assess environmental pollutants—just as Catherine's lost career put a human face on racism.

Long remarried—to another Catholic activist—Dad, Owen Shrader, is the original self-made man. A math whiz and self-described "tinkerer," he is a completely self-taught mechanical engineer, without a college degree. Beginning as a machinist, then becoming a tool-and-die maker, he worked his way up. He read voraciously, haunted the library, asked questions, learned from others, and never saw a problem he could not eventually solve. Now retired from General Electric, Dad spent most of his life supervising scores of university-trained engineers. His brilliance has ensured that, decades after his retirement, GE is still asking for his help and trying to send him to various locations abroad to solve the company's engineering and manufacturing problems. His standards, however, often irritated less meticulous engineers. At least twice when I was young, I recall Dad's arriving home from work and reporting to Mom that GE was sending him to (what he called) "charm school." Laughing, he explained that company vice-presidents were trying to teach him to "manipulate" the truth, to "sugarcoat" his demands for quality. Extravagantly generous and compassionate toward the "have-nots," Dad always expected the "haves" to behave in ways that were appropriate to their privileges. "Outspoken" is too mild a word to describe him.

Ever since the family moved to Fern Creek in the 1950s, Dad has been grafting vines, making wine from his own grapes, doing organic gardening, and raising most of the family vegetables. In 2007, he harvested eighty bushels of grapes. A vigorous eighty-six, Dad is still a powerful swimmer. He learned to snorkel in his late seventies, after his children took him on their scuba-diving trips. Each week he still volunteers, repairing Braille writers at the state School for the Blind. In his red Alfa Romeo convertible, he still drives local senior-home residents—all older than he—to their weekly medical appointments.

Abandoned by his father when he was a baby, Dad went with his mother to live with his grandmother. Speaking of his childhood, he says that sometimes he had only an apple to eat for the entire day. Yet he always describes himself as fortunate, partly because of Mr. Hukenbeck, a kindly Boy Scout leader, and partly because of Saint Xavier. In exchange for tuition, every day Dad cleaned all the classrooms at Saint X, the best Catholic high school in Louisville. Through his scout camping trips, led by Mr. Hukenbeck, Dad discovered both his long-standing love of wilderness and his dream of buying (and building on) rural land. Although he grew up in an inner-city slum, through scouting Dad learned the names of nearly every local bird, insect, tree, and flower. He also learned how to build or repair almost anything. Mr. Hukenbeck inspired Dad, became a father to him, and also helped him become an Eagle Scout. Several years ago, Dad gave one of his grandsons, Eric (Maurice's and my elder child), his faded-ribboned Eagle badge when Eric too received the award.

Just as Mom became Catherine to African-American girls in Newburg, Dad became Mr. Hukenbeck to many abandoned boys. For thirty years Dad ran the Boy Scout troop at Louisville's Saint Joseph Orphanage. Along with his own sons, Dad took the Saint Joseph's scouts on many long camping trips. Eager for them to experience wilderness, Dad said the experience would change their lives. During Dad's decades of scouting at the orphanage, its Roman Catholic sisters often would send home with him children who needed special attention. Although he and Mom already had six children of their own, three of these newer children—Vince, Janice, and Vickie—spent much of their childhoods with us. Dad and

Mom formally adopted Vickie, the youngest of our new brothers and sisters.

My favorite childhood memory of Dad is his leading family camping trips. Every summer in the 1950s and 1960s—after he had loaded Army-surplus tents, sleeping bags, canteens, tarps, two Coleman stoves, ice chests, and food into our flatbed trailer—our van and trailer headed for a different national park. On at least one trip, to Colorado and New Mexico, my youngest brother and sister were still in diapers. Dad and Mom led us everywhere—riding horseback in the Rockies, listening to park-ranger tales at desert campfires, or pitching tents in the driving rains of Hatteras. Those trips marked us for life. Dad and Mom made it possible for me to love the Canyonlands rim trail, or the Snake River whitewater, the way I love the lands that I call home. They made it possible for me to love diving the wall off Maui, or Molasses Reef off Key Largo, the way I love the pages of my favorite books. They made the Earth my treasure.

Cesar Chavez used to say that the best books are people's lives. My parents' lives were my books, more central than any I used in doing my doctoral degree and later writing. From them, especially Dad, I learned—and have passed on—the importance of early and direct experiences in nature. From them, especially Mom, I learned—and have passed on—a commitment to social-justice activism. Just as my brothers and sisters and I sometimes complained about our parents' activism and outspokenness, our (Maurice's and my) children used to complain that we were not like "normal" families. Instead of staying at home to have traditional holidays, we would pack the children and the scuba gear, head for the Keys, and spend days in, on, and under the water. Instead of turkey and dressing, our holiday dinners would be grilled fish and margaritas, consumed in the open air after a long day of diving.

Once Eric and Danielle started college, their days with us were brief, leaving no time for these family-holiday scuba trips. On one of their first visits home from Princeton, they sat glumly at the table, a Thanksgiving feast before them. Finally Danielle spoke up: "You know, since we aren't diving in the Keys, it doesn't really feel like Thanksgiving. Do you think there's time to pack the gear into the car?"

The principles that led my parents—especially Mom—to work for civil rights and to study liberation theology also inspired my own career in environmental justice and in (what I call) "liberation science." (Liberation science consists of pro bono mathematical and empirical analyses of pollution effects. Aimed at empowering and protecting the most vulnerable members of society, it uses scientific methods to reveal how deadly pollution often is disproportionately imposed on poor people, minorities, and children. It also shows how polluters frequently misuse science in order to try to justify these unfair burdens.) Seven years after Mom's death, my students and I faced our first pro bono environmental-justice battle. Armed with degrees in mathematics and philosophy of science, I helped do the science that led to shutting down a leaking nuclear dump that was destroying the lands and health of Appalachian subsistence farmers.

That experience led me to do postdoctoral work in hydrogeology, to learn how and when radioactive leachate can travel through subsurface water. Other controversies, in which polluters claimed that economics prevented them from cleaning up their messes, led me to do a second round of postdoctoral work, this time in economics. Still other investigations, into how to restore land once it was polluted, led me to do my third stint of postdoctoral work, in biology. As a result, liberation science has taken my students and me from helping solve hazardous-waste problems in equatorial Africa to planning nuclear dumps in Sweden, to protecting Native American lands in the Southwest, to studying the polluted neighborhoods of largely Latino and African-American communities in south Chicago.

More than a decade ago, my students and I celebrated the first major environmental-justice victory in the United States. In 1994, we had begun pro bono work with other scholars and Sierra Club attorneys. Our victory? We helped stop a multinational corporation from building a dangerous, unwanted, substandard uranium-enrichment facility in the poverty-ridden African-American community of Homer, Louisiana. Today Notre Dame students and I take on fifteen to twenty pro bono projects a year, mostly in the United

States. These range from showing the inadequate cleanup of chemical contamination in (largely African-American) East St. Louis, to analyzing flawed waste-dump plans for the lands of the Pala Band of Mission Indians in California. Last year we helped initiate laws requiring recycling of mercury-containing switches in Pennsylvania.

Cesar Chavez promised that, after a day on the picket lines, people would never be the same. My dream is that, after being baptized into an environmental-justice project, our students—and their view of religion—will never be the same. That dream is coming true. Many students have volunteered for Peace Corps work in Africa and Latin America. Some are organizing migrant workers in Florida camps. Others are getting medical degrees and hoping to serve in developing nations. Many have gone into environmental law. Still others are getting graduate degrees in environmental and public health, to prepare for government service. Almost universally, they say their university environmental-justice work changed their lives and their career plans.

For many of these students, for me, and for my parents, our Catholic faith has been one of the engines driving these efforts. Dad has a profound sense of the Earth as sacred, given by God. Mom saw herself as following the biblical imperatives to serve the poor and the powerless. For both of them, their dreams and their work were ways of keeping faith with their own Roman Catholic social-justice traditions, with the activism of Pope Leo XIII and his 1891 demand to recognize human rights, and with leaders like Berrigan, Chavez, Day, and others.

For me, doing liberation-science and environmental-justice work is not mainly about battles and successes. It is about keeping faith with these same family traditions; keeping faith with my parents and their care for others and for the Earth; and keeping faith with what it is to be human. Cesar Chavez believed that we become human only when we dedicate ourselves to someone in greater need, only when we choose to use our lives for others to bring about a better world—even if we don't always succeed.

Kristin Shrader-Frechette is the O'Neill Family Endowed Professor at the University of Notre Dame, where she teaches both in biological sciences and in philosophy. The author of fifteen books and more than 350 scholarly articles, she has advised the U.S. government, many foreign nations, and the United Nations on nuclear-waste disposal, standards for ionizing radiation, and environmental justice. Her books and articles have been translated into thirteen languages, and the U.S. National Science Foundation has funded her scientific research for twenty-five years. Shrader-Frechette's latest book, from Oxford University Press, is Taking Action, Saving Lives *(2007). In October 2007,* Catholic Digest *named her as one of twelve U.S. "heroes," whose faith has inspired them to serve others.*

Confessions of an Evangelical Tree Hugger

Matthew Sleeth

Sometimes we must lose ourselves in order to find our way.

I live in a small college town near Lexington, Kentucky. One summer, my wife and I and a couple of friends were invited to share the evening with a group of families who dwell together in an intentional manner, about sixty miles from our home.

The road there narrows from four to two to even fewer lanes. A blue mailbox comes up on the right. Make a left, and then proceed up the drive, whose high spots are blazed by the low-hanging undercarriage of cars like mine.

A dog comes up to greet us. Overdressed for these hot evenings, he pants and accepts a rub on the brow and a scratching behind the ears. I watch his tail sweep arcs of canine fellowship on the dusty ground.

Adults come out to greet us, and their children appear from places in the yard and barn. These children are different.

Their point of intersection with life is not a touchpad or a screen. Because the adults in their lives are worried about the death of nature, they are raising their children close to it.

It quickly becomes clear that these families spend much of their days in the woods, meadows, and gardens that surround this small cluster of homes. Children cannot protect what they do not know; they will not give up their convenience, much less their way of life, for what they do not love. I realize that these children are being raised as the guardians of tomorrow.

Before we break bread, Margie (one of the adults) takes us on a tour. She points to the roof of their home. Its long axis points south. The sun riseth, and goeth down, and hastens toward its zenith in the summer. In winter, when the sun is lower in the sky, it comes in their south-facing windows and provides free heat.

The term *eavesdrop* comes from hiding under the eaves of the house to listen surreptitiously to conversation. This is an eavesdropping home, but the conversation to be overheard is the chatter of rain. It flows from gutter to downspout to a cistern under the back porch. It is pumped up into the kitchen sink to wash dishes and then flows to the gray-water tank. Then the rain continues its journey downhill to the garden, where it hydrates the interstitial spaces in the lettuce of our salad, which we wash in the sink before dinner.

"How do you do it? How do you keep things going?" I ask this group of young and old, married and single, Catholic and Protestant people. The Lutheran pastor among them understands: I'm not asking about technology or the lack of it.

"We pray."

Prayer: it is what has brought them through the beginning years of adjustment to living in community; through the illnesses, the job changes, and the roller-coaster ride of children entering their teen years.

"We share the legacy of the people raised to live alone but needing each other."

"How?" I press.

"We'll show you, if you'd like to join us," they offer.

After dinner we retire to a room set aside as a chapel for vespers—one prayer book for every two people, a "novice" partnered with a community member. Hands slip back and forth between pages. Our collective voices sing songs written by French monks. We close with a period of free-form prayer, giving thanks, praying for mercy, and asking for help.

Outside, the children run about capturing grasshoppers, crickets, and other jumping things between cupped hands. Those creatures do not escape by the explosive movements of muscles coiled in their legs, but by quietly crawling through the whistle gap between the children's thumbs.

Inside the chapel there is a moment of quiet. We sit with God and tilt the ears of our souls toward the eternal voice of reason. On the wall hang a crucifix bearing Christ's body and a simple, unadorned cross, both symbols of suffering and triumph.

For my part, I accept both. It is not by accident that Christ died on a tree, nor that he worked with wood in his father's shop. Nor is it a coincidence that the word *tree* is mentioned more than five hundred times in the Bible. The human story begins with the tree of life in the garden. The last chapter of the Bible tells of two trees of life and an unpolluted river that flows between them. The leaves of these trees, we are told, will heal the nations.

It took us a thousand years to prove this biblical truth: that trees are, indeed, the breath of life. The transfer of life-giving gas from tree to human is not intuitive. Only in relatively recent human history was it discovered that oxygen comes not from rocks but from trees and photosynthesis.

God is not subtle about his feeling for trees. "I love the tall cedars," saith the Lord. Abraham plants an oak. The symbol of Christ's birthday is a conifer. We decorate them and sing, "O Christmas tree." Essays are made by fools like me, but only God can make a tree. The kingdom of heaven is "like a tree," Jesus said. So, yes, call me a tree hugger. So was my Lord.

The prayer service is over; dinner dishes are washed, dried, and put away. We take a last look around for the breadbasket and food containers that go back to our house, make one last trip to the composting toilets, and get into our hybrid car, quietly crunching gravel under tire. Crickets call to each other, and we say our good-byes. At the bottom of the driveway, I decide to follow the global positioning system rather than retrace our path. The robotic voice tells me to turn left, not right, at the blue mailbox. Despite the lessons of the evening, I put my confidence in satellites and microchips instead of evening stars and friends.

The GPS takes us on the shortest path, which includes crossing the Kentucky River on the Valley View ferry. What the GPS does not know is that the ferry man is gone for the night and will not return till morning. We have no map—just a computer showing this impassable way. I fall back on the stars. We need to head toward the nebula in Orion's belt, and then turn left at some point. On a dark single-lane road, I stop the car three-quarters of a mile past the last farmhouse to get my bearings.

We all step out and are at once baptized in the beauty of the place. Heaven will have no far-off highways roaring like oceans. It will be quiet, like these fields. The one on the left is cut and raked and ready for bailing. The hay on the right is waist high. Over both levitate the intermittently glowing abdomens of fireflies. Their luminescence joins up with the quiet, gentle chorus of the stars. The music of the spheres is a symphony, and the soloist tonight is the half-lit face of Sister Moon. She faces her brother the sun from a sidereal vantage point and hums a lullaby into the deep blue, star-filled heavens.

How strong is this faith and Bible I cling to? They have taken the families we visited from talk to action. They have planted a seed in my heart, to make me ache for nights filled with the peace of wild things in hedgerows, to make me long for the thousands of similar fields that have been plowed and planted with houses.

The fence in front of me wears a sign. It is too dim to read, but I imagine what it would say if Jesus owned this farm: Trespass gently. If your stomach is empty, come and share the harvest. If your spirit is hungry, come and pray.

C. S. Lewis, beloved creator of the Narnia series of books, says that if you know you are going down the wrong path, the shortest way to get back on track is to turn around and retrace your steps. We pile into the Prius, keeping the windows down so that we can smell the freshly cut hay as long as possible. Conversation dwindles, and fireflies continue to flicker behind the closed eyelids of my passengers.

We arrive home near midnight, saying a prayer of thanks before going our separate ways: Thank you for fields and fireflies and friendship. Thank you for faulty computers and the flawless beauty of your creation. Thank you for detours.

Sometimes we must lose ourselves in order to find our way.

Matthew Sleeth, MD, is the author of Serve God, Save the Planet: A Christian Call to Action *(www.servegodsavetheplanet.org) and executive director of Blessed Earth.*

Grace

Gary Snyder

There is a verse chanted by Zen Buddhists called the "Four Great Vows." The first line goes: "Sentient beings are numberless, I vow to save them." *Shujōmuhen seigando.* It's a bit daunting to announce this intention—aloud—to the universe daily. This vow stalked me for several years and finally pounced: I realized that I had vowed to let the sentient beings save me. In a similar way, the precept against taking life, against causing harm, doesn't stop in the negative. It is urging us to *give* life, to *undo* harm.

Those who attain some ultimate understanding of these things are called "buddhas," which means "awakened ones." The word is connected to the English verb *to bud*. I once wrote a little parable:

WHO THE BUDDHAS ARE

All the beings of the universe are already realized. That is, with the exception of one or two beings. In those rare cases the cities, villages, meadows, and forests, with all their birds, flowers, animals, rivers, trees, and humans, that surround such a person, all collaborate to educate, serve, challenge, and instruct such a one, until that person also becomes a New Beginner Enlightened Being. Recently realized beings are enthusiastic to teach and train and start schools and practices. Being able to do this develops their confidence and insight up to the point that they are fully ready to join the seamless world of interdependent play. Such new enlightened beginners are called "Buddhas" and they like to say things like "I am enlightened together with the whole universe" and so forth.

Boat in a Storm, 1987

Good luck! one might say. The test of the pudding is in the *eating*. It narrows down to a look at the conduct that is entwined with food. At mealtime (seated on the floor in lines) the Zen monks chant:

> Porridge is effective in ten ways
> To aid the student of Zen
> No limit to the good result
> Consummating eternal happiness

and

> Oh, all you demons and spirits
> We now offer this food to you
> May all of you everywhere
> Share it with us together

and

> We wash our bowls in this water
> It has the flavor of ambrosial dew
> We offer it to all demons and spirits
> May all be filled and satisfied
> *Om makula sai svaha*

And several other verses. These superstitious-sounding old ritual formulas are never mentioned in lectures, but they are at the heart of the teaching. Their import is older than Buddhism or any of the world religions. They are part of the first and last practice of the wild: *Grace.*

Everyone who ever lived took the lives of other animals, pulled plants, plucked fruit, and ate. Primary people have had their own ways of trying to understand the precept of non-harming. They knew that taking life required gratitude and care. There is no death that is not somebody's food, no life that is not somebody's death. Some would take this as a sign that the universe is fundamentally flawed. This leads to a disgust with self, with humanity, and with nature. Otherworldly philosophies end up doing more damage to the planet (and human psyches) than the pain and suffering that is in the existential conditions they seek to transcend.

The archaic religion is to kill god and eat him. Or her. The shimmering food-chain, the food-web, is the scary, beautiful condition of the biosphere. Subsistence people live without excuses.

The blood is on your own hands as you divide the liver from the gallbladder. You have watched the color fade on the glimmer of the trout. A subsistence economy is a sacramental economy because it has faced up to one of the critical problems of life and death: the taking of life for food. Contemporary people do not need to hunt, many cannot even afford meat, and in the developed world the variety of foods available to us makes the avoidance of meat an easy choice. Forests in the tropics are cut to make pasture to raise beef for the American market. Our distance from the source of our food enables us to be superficially more comfortable, and distinctly more ignorant.

Eating is a sacrament. The grace we say clears our hearts and guides the children and welcomes the guest, all at the same time. We look at eggs, apples, and stew. They are evidence of plenitude, excess, a great reproductive exuberance. Millions of grains of grass-seed that will become rice or flour, millions of codfish fry that will never, and *must* never, grow to maturity. Innumerable little seeds are sacrifices to the food chain. A parsnip in the ground is a marvel of living chemistry, making sugars and flavors from earth, air, water. And if we do eat meat it is the life, the bounce, the swish, of a great alert being with keen ears and lovely eyes, with foursquare feet and a huge beating heart that we eat, let us not deceive ourselves.

We too will be offerings—we are all edible. And if we are not devoured quickly, we are big enough (like the old down trees) to provide a long, slow meal to the smaller critters.

Whale carcasses that sink several miles deep in the ocean feed organisms in the dark for fifteen years. (It seems to take about two thousand to exhaust the nutrients in a high civilization.)

At our house we say a Buddhist grace—

> We venerate the Three Treasures [teachers, the wild, and
>   friends]
> And are thankful for this meal
> The work of many people
> And the sharing of other forms of life.

Anyone can use a grace from their own tradition (and really give it meaning)—or make up their own. Saying some sort of grace is never inappropriate, and speeches and announcements can be tacked onto it. It is a plain, ordinary old-fashioned little thing to do that connects us with all our ancestors.

> A monk asked Dong-shan: "Is there a practice for people
> to follow?" Dong-shan answered: "When you become a
> real person, there is such a practice."

Sarvamangalam, Good Luck to All.

Gary Snyder grew up in the Pacific Northwest, where he worked on the family farm and graduated from Reed College in Portland in 1951. He did mountaineering, seasonal Forest Service work, and logging. He did graduate study in linguistics at Indiana University and at the University of California,

Berkeley, in the Department of East Asian Languages. During his Bay Area years, Snyder was part of the San Francisco Poetry Renaissance. In 1956 he moved to Kyoto, Japan, to study Buddhism and East Asian culture, returning to North America in 1969.

For the last thirty-eight years, Snyder has lived in Nevada County, in a handmade house near the Yuba River. He has traveled widely: lecturing, giving poetry readings, and doing workshops on ecological, Buddhist, and community matters. He has published eighteen books of prose and poetry and won a Pulitzer Prize and a Bollingen Prize for his work. On the home terrain, with the Yuba Watershed Institute, he is focusing on sustainable forestry and community interactions with public land. Snyder's most recent book is Back on the Fire, essays that link Buddhism, environmentalism, and local practice.

In the Beginning, Eden

Phyllis Tickle

One of the genuine pleasures of the writing life, ironically enough, is not writing at all; rather, it is the business of speaking directly and in real time to audiences. For a writer like me, who is by area of expertise a professional religionist, those audiences usually are made up of other religionists, most commonly of practicing clergy, their professional support staffs, deeply involved and committed laity, or any combination of these. But sometimes, blessedly, the audience is an auditorium full of undergraduates and the occasion an endowed lecture of one sort or another.

While one always learns something in any public engagement with any audience, what one learns in the course of engaging a group of healthy, lively undergraduates is, more often than not, opinion-changing and mind-expanding. More to the point, it unfailingly gives birth to at least one poignant story or one simple but brilliant insight or one gentle conviction still too new to be tarnished by overmuch handling. Very rarely, an endowed lecture will deliver up all three in one fell swoop. I had one of those rare experiences recently.

I was giving a set of lectures at an urban college in the Midwest. When the talk and question-and-answer session were over, a few students and faculty gathered, as they always do, around the podium to carry the discussion into a more personal and candid wind-down. Although this audience did include some graduate students and seminarians, one of those who came that last afternoon was clearly an undergraduate, most probably, I thought, a freshman. From her self-effacement and decorum of earnest unease, I guessed as well that college had been her first intimate experience of life in the city.

She had two other students with her, and together they hung back, listening to the discussion and waiting until everyone else had drifted away. The three of them seemed to be very close in affection and also in their shared concerns, but my freshman was obviously their leader and spokeswoman. Could they ask me one last question, she wanted to know. I said, of course, and almost immediately realized that what she wanted to express was not so much a question as the perfect self-articulation I had come hoping to hear when I spoke about the Christian life in the twenty-first century.

What she actually said was, "I want somebody to tell me where I stop." She shrugged her shoulders, and the boy in the group poked her to go on. She tried again. "What I mean is that I don't know anymore where I end.

"Am I just inside my skin, sort of interior to it, you know? Or am I just what's on the inside side of my underwear and clothes? Or am I as far out as my aura, because," she added rather apologetically, "there really is an aura around all of us, or so our psych prof says, anyway.

"Or am I, like, only just 'here' in among us three, because we really do hang together all the time?

"Or am I out in all of this?" and she gave a kind of feeble but all-encompassing sweep of her hand toward the auditorium behind us. Then she shrugged again, almost in defeat, and there was a kind of break in her voice.

"I just want to know where I stop, that's all . . . where I aren't any more."

I don't know whether it was her earnestness or her slip of grammar that most endeared that girl-child to me in that moment; but either way, there was no doubting the sincerity of her desire to be answered. One can say that what she was asking was basically an existential question. But one must also say that her existential experience was as valid as it was painful. On the farm—it turned out to be a dairy farm, by the way— she had known where she "stopped." She didn't, in other words. That is, on the farm, she simply did not "stop."

As far as the eye could see and as far as the imagination could reach, she was; for she and the Earth by whose rules she lived were part and parcel of one another. She rose in accord with her father's cows, who rose in accord with the demands of their milk making. She tended animals in accord with the seasons of the Earth and of their bodies, which were part of it; and the ebb and flow of both determined the ebb and flow of her own. She knew herself to be no more than a cog in a magnificent machine, but she also knew that the machine was immense and total, and that, by function and connection, she was totally vulnerable, ultimately powerless, and because of these things totally borderless. She was, in effect, the quintessential expression of a rural understanding of Earth.

I, too, am rural. Or, like my young inquisitor, I once lived rural and still think rural. The farm we worked and ate off of for years was beef, not dairy, and family-size small, not working-size large. And though my husband and I still live on a considerable portion of that same land, we no longer make any pretense of farming it. Our barn molders away in the hot west Tennessee sun, each passing season taking a bit more of its paint or its siding or its tin roofing. No cows have grazed our fields in over a decade, and only bush-hogging with a heavy-duty mower keeps our pastures open now. The kitchen garden still feeds us well in the summers, but I no longer do any preserving or canning or freezing against the winter's short supplies. Without children to feed and without children to teach, it seems pointless. They learned while they were with us and while they ate the products of their own hands. Like us, they still think rural, even though some of our seven no longer live that way.

All that said, one still must move very cautiously when it comes to any discussion about the habits and mind-sets involved in thinking rural. Especially in America, the phrase "thinking rural" should never be bandied about casually or without annotation. For a people whose forebears were almost all farm-bound in lifestyle and income, and for a nation whose land mass is huge and mostly farmed or kept fallow, we twenty-first-century Americans have an almost paradoxical tendency to romanticize rurality. And once something is romanticized, it is effectually relegated to the precious and removed from the operative and informative.

There is nothing romantic or even particularly *ennobling* about getting welts all over one's hands from picking okra and corn, or bruises from being jostled by hungry cows, or stiff bones from shoveling manure. What there is, however, is a subtle but pervasive sense of citizenship in the world as it is. There is the borderlessness of my freshman, her humanizing acceptance of vulnerability, and her assumption of oneness in substance and rhythm with the immediate environment— *immediate* being defined for her as a certain, unimpeded vastness that she could walk freely upon.

The shock for the rural thinker turned city dweller is in discovering that the city lives not on the earth but above it by several layers of mechanical and technological remove. The urban dweller (who quickly becomes an urban thinker) uses the treasures of Earth not to perpetuate and preserve it but to serve and facilitate the life of the city. The rural thinker stands small in a grandeur he or she must accommodate to constantly. The urban thinker stands on a stage he or she has cut to size, and then, standing there, dares to write the play.

Neither side of that divide in thinking and perceiving is inherently superior to or worse than the other. There is nothing quaint or impractical or regressive about rural values any more than there is something malevolent or noxious or destructive about urbanization per se. Condemning postmodern urban life is in many ways just another, albeit more negative, form of romanticization, and just as deplorable.

Likewise, there is nothing fundamentally deleterious to a human being about having to make the existential shifts required in moving from rural to urban living. What is wrong is our current inability or outright unwillingness to balance, meld, and employ simultaneously both ways of seeing the Earth and both ways of addressing the environment. Embedded in the earnestness of our current concerns is a kind of partisan entrenchment on both sides. There are substantial differences between addressing conservation ecology with intent to govern the Earth and addressing conservation ecology with intent to be as one with it, yet each side of the argument is loath to make room for much discussion of those differences. But for me, as a practicing Christian and a professional religionist, environmental arguments based on either common sense or enlightened self-interest will always be, at best, secondary or tertiary ones.

When I say I am a practicing Christian, what I am saying, among other things, is that like a large part of the Earth's population—the larger part, in fact—I am what technically is called an Abrahamic, or, put another way, a member of the Abrahamic faiths. That is, Jews, Christians, and Muslims alike all claim a common spiritual forebear in Abraham. As such, we hold in common the part of Torah that is the story of human experience from the creation itself to Abraham's call to sacrifice his son to God. In that foundational bit of shared religious heritage, the dominant stories for us are the opening and closing ones—the Creation and the aborted Sacrifice. In both stories, a great gift is given to humanity and an order to reverence God is established. It is the ordering of the Torah creation story, however, that every observant Abrahamic, whether farmer, suburbanite, or industrialist, is called to honor first when he or she speaks about environmental issues.

For Abrahamics, the great gift in Eden was that of receiving soul, of our birthing as creatures formed in the image of God. But there was a prior gift that enabled the great gift. There was Eden. Only after God's formation of a context for the soul's well-being were *we* formed.

Both the rural and the urban dweller recognize, albeit in different ways, that creation is a tool, a gift to be enjoyed, and a means to be employed; but for the observant Jew or Christian or

Muslim, Earth exists neither to be deified nor to be consumed. Rather, it exists now, as it has from the beginning, as teacher, limitation, and purposed circumstance. It is a nursery of sorts, an incubator, in which each of us may first uncurl, then stretch, and finally rise up into the business of growing holy before God. From the Abrahamic point of view, whatever we humans plot to do with and to the Earth is always to be measured by what the pursuit of such an action will do to human souls and their progress toward living fully into the image of God. And I would submit that, in the final analysis, such a gauge is the only sustainable one, simply because it alone is a benison upon all God's peoples, whether they be Abrahamic or not.

By this I mean that my freshman, as I told her, did not and does not "end." My faith teaches instead that she, like all of us, is a piece and a part of all of us—a cell among cells in an organic whole, a plotline among myriad plotlines in a mystery that, ironically, is most mysterious to itself. Find her borders and boundaries? No, probably not. But I pray God that my young inquisitor will come in time to love with totality their diffuseness; for then she will have come in time to have learned to love all of us. That, after all, is the great benison.

Sixteenth Week of Ordinary Time, 2007

Phyllis Tickle is an authority on religion in America and a sought-after lecturer on the subject. She was founding editor of the Religion Department of Publishers Weekly, *the international journal of the book industry*, and is frequently quoted in major print and electronic media. In addition to her numerous essays, articles, and interviews, Tickle is the author of more than two dozen books on religion and spirituality, most notably the Divine Hours series of manuals for observing fixed-hour prayer.

Tickle began her career as a college teacher and served as academic dean to the Memphis College of Art before entering full-time into writing and publishing. Her work has been honored by the book industry's Mays Award for lifetime achievement in writing and publishing, an honorary degree of Doctor of Humane Letters from the Berkeley Divinity School at Yale University, and a Lifetime Achievement Award from the Christy Awards organization. Tickle is currently a Senior Fellow of Cathedral College of the Washington National Cathedral. A founding member of the Canterbury Roundtable and a lay eucharistic minister and lector in the Episcopal Church, Tickle is the mother of seven children and, with her physician-husband, makes her home on a small farm in Lucy, Tennessee.

When Abraham Sees God in Oak Trees

Arthur Waskow

One of the important portions of the Torah that speak of Abraham and his family (Genesis 18:1 through 22:24) is traditionally read in synagogues on the Shabbat and is called Vayeira, from its first word. This word is usually translated as "appeared," but it comes from the root for "see," and the same root appears in a different form right afterward.

The second word is "YHWH," one of the crucial names of God. This name is usually translated as "the Lord," but this comes from the traditional Jewish practice of deliberately substituting the word *adonai* ("Lord") instead of trying to pronounce the strange four-letter name. Since this sacred unpronounceable name with no vowels can be "pronounced" only by breathing—"*Yyyyhhhhwwwwhhhh*"—I translate it as "the breath of life" or "the wind/breath/spirit of the world."

The first sentence says, "YHWH brought-about-being-seen to [Abraham] in [*b'*] the oaks of Mamre." Then the story continues: "And he lifted up his eyes and saw [*va'yar*], and here!—three people were standing upon him, and he saw [*va'yar*] and ran . . . [to bring-them-near and then to feed them]."

First the oak trees themselves and then the three visitors are the visible, see-able presence of God.

How can the Divine Breathing-Spirit of the world become visible in trees? Think about the rustling leaves, quivering as the wind rushes from them, in them, into them. Quivering as the trees breathe out what we breathe in (oxygen), and then breathe in what we breathe out (carbon dioxide). This is the rhythm of life on our planet. As we open our eyes to this rush of breath, we see God.

It was not until Abraham saw God breathing in these oak trees that Abraham was able to see God breathing in human beings.

For just after experiencing God in the trees, as Abraham sees travelers arriving, as he rushes to greet and feed them, he and Sarah recognize these visitors as messengers from God. (We call them "angels," but the Hebrew word and its Greek translation, *angelos*, simply mean "messenger.") So he and Sarah act to affirm the holiness they now can see, by feeding God, who, of course, is never visible except in all that is around us. That is, is *always* visible if we open our eyes. Feeding God by feeding human beings—sharing with earthy human beings the abundance of the Earth.

And in response, the human beings who are God's messengers tell the aged Abraham and Sarah that they will, after all, have a child.

Once Abraham had deeply seen the interbreathing of all life as God, he more deeply saw the intertwining of *adam* and *adamah*, the human earthlings and the earthy humus—the intertwining that feeds us all and celebrates the One. Not until he saw God in this body of earth-human interchange could his and Sarah's bodies intertwine to seed new life.

Until then, Sarah had been an *akarah*—a "root" without a sprouting. Perhaps it was not she who was barren; perhaps her rootedness needed some new quickening in Abraham, some vision more connected to the Earth, to make her root more fruitful.

So if this story honors the first expression of eco-Judaism (and maybe eco-Christianity and eco-Islam, all born of Abraham's vision), we should honor the story by opening our eyes to its fullness.

Look closely at a tree. Sniff at its leaves, each sniff a moment of breathing life into it and out of it. Pray not to the tree but to the whispering, rustling Breath that enters it and leaves it.

Promise to sustain it. Act to sustain it.

Rabbi Arthur Waskow is director of the Shalom Center (www.shalom ctr.org), which voices a new prophetic agenda for Jewish, multireligious, and American life and sponsors the Green Menorah Covenant campaign to embody eco-Judaism in Jewish practice and advocacy. He is the author or editor of Down-to-Earth Judaism; Torah of the Earth; Trees, Earth, and Torah; and other books that reinterpret Jewish festivals, life-spiral ceremonies, and Torah from an eco-Jewish perspective.

God, Nature, and the Great Unraveling

Terry Tempest Williams

For Louis Gakumba, December 31, 2007

When it comes to God and Nature, I consult my priest in all things common, Walt Whitman. In "To a President," he writes, "All you are doing and saying is to America dangled mirages, / You have not learn'd of Nature—of the politics of Nature you / have not learn'd the great amplitude, rectitude, impartiality, / You have not seen that only such as they are for these States, / And that what is less than they must sooner or later lift off from these States."

Religion offered me a mirage, a belief I took as truth. Whatever I was walking toward remained an illusive bet on the horizon, shimmering and wet. Mormonism embodied both a spiritual life and a cultural identity. Conformity created community, and in community we were safe. To the outside world we were peculiar, but in our world the Church of Jesus Christ of Latter-day Saints was a normal state of being. It was a theology born out of the hungry prayers of a fourteen-year-old boy in search of God, practiced a hundred and fifty years later by a pragmatic people who believe that America is a sacred geography. Joseph Smith received the vision and translated it into the Book of Mormon. Brigham Young brought the vision west and sought the desert as a refuge against persecution. This is the place where we chose to settle as a people—on the remote shores of an inland sea in the Great Basin. Mirages are common: a destination never to be reached, only a liquid lie to follow all the way to the horizon, another name for hope.

In church, I believed what I was told: *We were a chosen people. Three kingdoms awaited us after death. We, too, could create our own worlds in partnership with our eternal mate.* But once outside, I wandered.

I wandered into my own backyard of scrub oak and sagebrush in the arid foothills of the Wasatch Mountains that rise above Salt Lake City. As children, my brother and I created our own game of Capture in which we were never caught and rarely seen, safely hidden inside our tree houses. The only compass point we needed was located in our imaginations. From an early age, truth was based on what I could see—rufous-sided towhees scratching in the understory of last year's leaves, lazuli buntings suspended as turquoise exclamation marks in a canopy of green, and blue-gray gnatcatchers with side-flicking tails playing the role of commas in an ongoing narrative of wild nature. Magpies, evening grosbeaks, scrub jays, and turkey vultures soaring overhead were expected visitors. Rattlesnakes were a cautionary tale: we heard them first, saw them coil second, and before counting to three, we ran. Change was spoken only through clouds.

One day when I was eight, playing in the oakbrush (as we called it), I spotted a white bird perched above me, a shock of light in a shadowed world. It was unlike anything I had ever seen. I ran inside and telephoned my grandmother, still watching the ghost bird through the sliding glass doors that faced the oaks. I explained that the size and shape of this mysterious bird were those of a robin, only without the brown back, black head, and red breast. She listened carefully. We both had our bird books in hand. "Perhaps it is an albino," she said, "a bird without pigmentation. Even the eyes are without color." That very word, *albino*, was a revelation to me. She might as well have said "of the spirit world," a concept Mormons understand.

We hung up, and I returned to watching this rare specimen in my own backyard. It was indeed a robin, the most common of birds, free of its prescribed dressings, white with red eyes. I was inspired and called her "the Holy Ghost."

When I reported my finding to our local Audubon chapter, the president said he could not legitimately count it as a "credible sighting" due to my age. My grandmother, on hearing this, simply shook her head and said, "Trust your instincts. The bird doesn't need to be counted and neither do you."

Each Sunday in church, a man dressed in a black suit walked slowly up the aisles, counting those of us in the congregation, row by row. Numbers mattered. We were a growing religion. Our religion keeps records and stores them in a mountain. To be a member of the Mormon faith means being counted. Yet, like the albino robin in the oakbrush, I felt more spirit than flesh and tried to remain invisible. And so, much of my childhood was spent outside, unseen, in the company of Whitman's three words: *amplitude, rectitude, impartiality.*

The American West has a natural amplitude, a breadth of range that extends from the Grand Tetons of the Northern Rockies to Great Salt Lake in the Great Basin to the red-rock canyons of southern Utah. I came to rely on this largeness of landscape and sky, and on the spiritual quadrants that ran north and south, east and west. When the Milky Way arched over our family in a summer's night sky, humility was not a word spoken but a sensation felt. Our human voice was silenced in the presence of a bugling elk. Prayers were sent on the backs of migrating birds, usually white pelicans flying in spiral columns like feathered DNA.

Rectitude I understood to be a strong moral integrity of character or actions. To locate it my brother and I looked no further than the deer we watched behind our home. Herds of deer remained hidden in the creases and gullies of the foothills. We sat amid the sage in stillness, until they surrounded us without fear. There was a gentleness we came to understand, alongside great strength and stamina, especially during winter. Their browse, twigs half covered in snow, became a kind of sacrament to us. Making contact with their large dark eyes informed my faith in a world both intimate and unfathomable.

From the desert I learned the power of impartiality. No water, no life. It didn't matter if you were a man, woman, or child; a frog, snake, or bat. If it rains, both animal and human can drink. A cactus blooms. Potholes appear like a liquid kiss, just long enough to quell a dry throat. Now you see them, now you don't. Water in the desert becomes a matter of faith. To be human in the desert is no advantage; a consciousness receives no favors in times of drought. We are all on equal footing: sand. And where water is not the great arbiter of justice, then geology is. A rockfall knows no mercy; if you are standing in the wrong place at the wrong time, you die. Wild nature is indifferent. It cares nothing for the sentiment of a bleeding heart. It was in the austerity of Utah's red-rock desert that I came to know God as a force of nature on Earth, not an exalted being levitating in heaven.

"You have not learn'd of Nature—of the politics of Nature. . . . And that what is less than they must sooner or later lift off from these States."

It feels quite simple, really, my allegiance to a natural mind over an institutional one. My path from a Latter-day Saint to a latter-day human has been, in its pleasure and struggle, like walking the gentle path of deer. The Holy Ghost I was taught to worship indoors has been replaced by the Holy Ghost I followed outside, even in the form of an albino robin, who asked me to consider the countenance of a species before its color.

Ascension has become for me a matter more closely aligned with wild iris than with Jesus. And when I want the prayers of my heart to be heard and carried, I go to the place of reversing tides in the Bay of Fundy, near the northern edge of Maine, to watch the ocean empty out and witness, for a few precious minutes, a small, shallow pool of stillness find its equilibrium. Then, as if led by a line of light, the incoming tide rushes in and fills the bay with an abundance of water and an exuberance that defies logic or faith. Twice daily, these tides are a testament to the ebb and flow of a dynamic will, pulled forward and back by the gravity and presence of the moon.

For me, religion is still a mirage in the desert—only now I no longer see it as a shimmering glint of hope on the horizon but as an abstraction of thought that I cannot hold. Neither does it hold me. The God I know is water—a dewdrop and a flood, a weeping rock wall, and the Atlantic in full swing, retreating one moment and rushing in the next. I feel the holy waves within my own body.

God is rain. God is drought. Earth is a revolving state of grace.

I believe in both God and nature. God in nature. God within the majesty of our own breathing, pulsating bodies. We are not separate. The God I have felt move me from the seat of certitude to the seat of my own heart translates to heat, the white-hot current that runs through all of us. The Great Unraveling inspires a letting go of all we have been taught, as our ego begins to untangle itself from what we have created to a deeper understanding of what has been created before us. This unlearned moment becomes our awakening. Earth underfoot replaces heaven above. Instead of trying to define the ineffable through our own images and count ourselves as members of a congregation in power, we can begin to live with the mysteries and humbly congregate around them with awe and wonder and respect.

Terry Tempest Williams was raised a fifth-generation Mormon within sight of Utah's Great Salt Lake. A naturalist and wilderness activist as well as an author, she has written widely on the American West, her own family, and what she calls "the open space of democracy." Among her best-known books are the memoir Refuge: An Unnatural History of Family *and* Place, Leap, *and* Red: Passion and Patience in the Desert. *She has also written two children's books and edited the collection* Testimony: Writers Speak on Behalf of Utah Wilderness. *Pantheon Books will publish her forthcoming book,* Finding Beauty in a Broken World, *in 2008. Williams is the Annie Clark Tanner Scholar in the Environmental Humanities graduate program at the University of Utah.*

Acknowledgments

The editors are deeply grateful, above all, to the contributors who lent their names, wisdom, and eloquence to this collection and cooperated so graciously with our editorial process. In addition, we wish to thank Sierra Club national publicist Orli Cotel for helping to hatch the idea for the book and Carl Pope, Sierra Club's executive director, for supporting the idea and writing the foreword. For facilitating our contacts with contributors, we would like to express our appreciation to the staff of the Ecumenical Patriarchate in Istanbul, Professor D. Giuseppe Costa at the Libreria Editrice Vaticana, Sarah Mattingly of Joel Hunter's office, Maryam Sirat (assistant to Dr. Seyyed Hossein Nasr), Joanna Blotner, Carl Brandt, Sam Carriere, Mohamad A. Chakaki, Emily Cook, Qaid Hassan, Mark Katz, Chris LaTondresse, Hisham Mahmoud, Bill Poole, Donald Schell, Nancy Sleeth, and Lori Thompson. And for their efforts on behalf of the project, we thank Robbie Cox, Susan Emmerich, Bonita Hurd, Rafael Reyes, and Jack Shoemaker.

We are grateful for the support of our colleagues at the Sierra Club who made it possible for us to work on this project: Kim Haddow, national communications director; Melanie Griffin, national director of Environmental Partnerships; and Helen Sweetland, publisher of Sierra Club Books.